There Once Was a Man Who Suffered

There Once Was a Man Who Suffered

The Book of Job in Limericks

SHARON ARPANA EDWARDS

CONSONANT
BOOKS

Published in the United States by Consonant Books
P. O. Box 236, Pasadena, CA 91102
sharonarpana.com

Library of Congress Control Number: 2022920723
ISBN: 978-0-9893233-9-0

BISAC Subject Headings:
RELIGION / Biblical Studies / Old Testament / Poetry &
Wisdom Literature
POETRY / Subjects & Themes / Inspirational & Religious
POETRY / Women Authors

Printed in the United States of America
FIRST EDITION

For Atish, Nihara,
Alita, Samaya, and Nihal:
May your light and momentary afflictions
achieve for you an eternal glory
that far outweighs them all.

So we do not focus on what is seen,
but on what is unseen.
For what is seen is temporary,
but what is unseen is eternal.
2 Corinthians 4:18

> Celestial light
> Shine inward, and the mind through all her powers
> Irradiate, there plant eyes, all mist from thence
> Purge and disperse, that I may see and tell
> Of things invisible to mortal sight.

—Milton, *Paradise Lost*, Book III

Contents

x   *Contents*

Introduction

Job's life is no laughing matter—but the limerick *is*. In fact, limericks are typically used for humor, satire, and even bawdiness. So why did I choose this lighthearted form of verse for the heaviest book of the Bible?

Strictly speaking, *it* chose *me*, as inspiration tends to do. But the idea appealed to me, so I said yes. Only later did I realize that this pithy, uncomplicated style could make the Book of Job more accessible to readers who find the original text forbidding, as I once did.

The night when poetry came a-calling I was laid up with a high fever, thinking of my younger nephew's seventeenth birthday celebrations underway in India. After texting him I rose to brush my teeth, when for no apparent reason I remembered this self-deprecating limerick from the past:

> There once was an Indian American
> Writer who wielded her pen
> Sometimes in jest
> To aid in her quest
> For foibles in women and men.

Unaware that God was about to give me the biggest surprise of my life, I recalled other limericks I had written for a lark. And suddenly this verse was rolling off my tongue:

> In the biblical land of Ur
> A man named Job did suffer
> No comfort was his wife
> Whom he'd married for life
> Or else he'd surely have left her.

I finished my ablutions with a chuckle and returned to bed. I wasn't chuckling when I opened my Bible next morning to discover that Job had dwelt in *Uz*, not *Ur*, where the patriarch Abraham had once lived.

Why I knew so little of the Book of Job even though I've been reading the Bible for almost half a century I have shared in the afterword. Suffice it to say here that when I read Job 1:1, it struck me in a flash of inspiration that I should tell Job's story in limericks.

The genre and timing of this book caught me by surprise. While I have long suspected I would someday write a book on suffering, I never dreamt it would be in limericks. And having lost my mother just eight months earlier, I wasn't planning to write *any* book at the time, let alone one like this.

I said yes to the idea because the limerick's clear-cut metric pattern and rhyme scheme made the mission seem possible. And although I was less familiar with the Book of Job than I should have been, I am no stranger to its central theme: the problem of human suffering.

I incurred deep emotional wounds in childhood, primarily through my father's alcoholism, verbal abuse, and occasional violence, and his rejection of me as a second daughter. In adulthood I have wandered in a vocational, locational, and relational wilderness, unable to make a living by writing or to find a place where I feel at home. And barring a brief bad marriage, I have spent my entire adult life in singlehood, at times even celebrating holidays on my own. A million solitary moments lie behind this stanza in the prologue:

> Why do some people find true love,
> A match made in heaven above,
> Whereas others yet
> Aren't able to get
> The partner they pray for and dream of?

Singleness has been pivotal in my formation as a writer and enriched me in a myriad of other ways, but it is not without its challenges. And although my relationship with my father was fully restored before he died and my childhood hurts are a thing of the past, I remain disabled by a congenital condition in my hands. Short of a miracle, which I believe is possible, I will have to live with physical pain and limitation for the rest of my life.

Thanks to my passion for prayer, I am also privy to the griefs of others. People have told me countless tales of woe, caused by a personal mistake, by someone else's actions, or by a seemingly random accident. I have lost my ability to be shocked but am always saddened to be reminded of the evil prevalent in this world.

Over the course of my editorial career, I have helped a number of writers tell stories of tragedy and loss. Shortly before this book came my way, I edited an essay for an international student who was applying for a graduate fellowship at Harvard. Raised in a war-torn African nation, this man had witnessed the sort of privation and terror no one should have to, least of all in youth.

As a reader I have vicariously experienced the ordeals of hundreds of fictional characters, for the best stories are about what Hamlet calls "the slings and arrows of outrageous fortune." The bildungsroman, a type of novel I enjoy, traces the moral and psychological development of a protagonist who must rise above especially *childhood* wounds, as Jane Eyre and Pip memorably do.

My own quest for inner healing commenced in my early twenties. I was making good progress when a breakup on the eve of my younger sister's wedding in 1993 triggered the first major crisis of my adulthood. Though crushing when it happened, in retrospect I can see how critical the event was to my emotional and spiritual growth. It stimulated vocational development as well, for I took to pouring out my pain on paper. The earliest poem composed during that season of tears was titled "Care."

> Sometimes I am afraid of the future
> What will tomorrow bring—
> Poverty or uncertainty,
> Pain or suffering?
>
> Then I consider the lilies of the field
> And the happy birds of the air—
> With faith and joy they live today,
> Unburdened with tomorrow's care.
>
> The Lord, who so arrays these flowers,
> And feeds the smallest sparrow,
> Cares daily for my every need—
> Why should I fear tomorrow![1]

On the very day of the breakup I threw myself into Scripture, discovering the beauties of Psalm 119 and the consolations of Lamentations 3 for the first time. Over the next several months I devoured every book I could find on suffering. The two that impacted me most profoundly were Corrie ten Boom's gut-wrenching Holocaust memoir, *The Hiding Place*, and an insightful volume by Theodore H. Epp titled *Why Do Christians Suffer?* Epp's analogy of the gold refining process taught me a key purpose of pain and has influenced a section in the epilogue.

At one point in this crucible I sensed the Lord assuring me He would use my trials to make me a woman of faith. I prayed that He would also let me write a book on faith someday. In my youthful exuberance, I was clueless as to how much suffering was required for my faith to be refined, and I never expected it to take *twenty-three* years!

This book on faith, *The Blessing of Melchizedek*, was my second; its predecessor was a collection of stories set in Los Angeles, where I had moved in 1999. Named for the street known as Little India, *Pioneer Boulevard* explores the themes of immigration and acculturation, both of which can be bewildering and extremely stressful. The difference is that whereas immigration ends when one acquires citizenship, acculturation can be lifelong. This has certainly been the case for me. Even though I was naturalized in 2005, at times I still feel like a stranger in a strange land.

When the 2020s dawned, I was bedridden after falling from the top of a defective stair master at the gym. The machine had not been marked out of order when I climbed on, and the fall severely injured my left side. Emotionally, I was reeling from a recent revelation about the congenital condition in my hands. The fact that I'd had nothing to do with either the defective stair master or the faulty gene forced me to confront a dilemma that has puzzled humanity since Cain killed Abel: the question of innocent suffering.

On the heels of my private grief, a fiery dart from hell known as coronavirus plunged the world into a collective sorrow. Among the numerous heartrending tales I heard in the early days, the one that utterly undid me was of the displaced migrant workers in northern India, where pregnant women walked barefoot for hundreds of miles to their villages, in the blazing heat of summer, and children ate grass and salt to survive.

Suffering of any kind is distressing, but the suffering of the vulnerable is on an altogether different level. To do my part, I raised funds for a nonprofit serving the migrant workers and kept them in my prayers, but their stories would haunt me for months.

As the lockdown progressed with its searing sense of isolation, I sustained injuries in a new set of accidents. In one my car was totaled; in another I again hurt my left side after slipping on black ice.

And then came the knockout punch.

In early May 2021, as coronavirus was wreaking fresh havoc in India, my mother died after a three-day hospitalization. Along with the trauma of losing her, I was shattered that my prayers for her healing had gone unanswered. Everyone else I had prayed for left the hospital alive, but my own mother left in a body bag, in an ambulance heading for the cemetery where she had buried my father in December 2009.

I spiraled into a vortex of despair in the weeks that followed. Although the Holy Spirit spoke to me through some significant dreams and perfectly timed scriptures, and while I still enjoyed praying for others, I lived with a dull, persistent ache. The counsel of my pastors and close friends did little to console me. I knew what they were saying was true, but my soul, as the psalmist candidly states, "refused to be comforted" (Ps. 77:2).

Sick at heart like never before, I steadily declined in health until eventually contracting the illness during which I received the idea for this book. Eight days after I started writing, I found myself in the emergency room with suspected heart trouble. I had begun the prologue's *Hamlet* stanzas that morning and was annoyed at the interruption. But since it is better to be than not to be, I submitted to the rigors of an ER visit.

The employee who checked me in decided I deserved triage status, so I was whisked off to have my vitals measured and various portions of my anatomy x-rayed and injected. Following a lengthy ultrasound to locate a vein in my right hand, I was informed that the needle would remain in place even after six vials were drawn, should more blood be required.

In this unenviable condition I was anticipating a peaceful nap in an exam room with dimmed lights. Instead, with one brusque command, I was cast into the outer brightness of the front lobby.

It was a busy evening in the ER, as if the entire city had simultaneously developed a medical emergency. Inserting my headphones, I began to pray for those around me who appeared to need it most. I also asked the Lord to let me encourage at least one of my fellow patients. My opportunity arrived shortly, when a stocky black-haired man entered the lobby in the throes of a panic attack.

Seeing him pace frantically, barely able to complete a sentence, I recalled a similar attack I'd had after a devastating breakup in 2009, and I discerned that this was the person I had to encourage. Once checked in, he stepped into the hallway where he could pace freely. I joined him and walked alongside, though more slowly.

Despite his anguish, Manuel (not his real name) listened as I shared how God had liberated me from years of depression, reciting verses as the Holy Spirit brought them to mind. I was in the midst of a quotation when he abruptly stopped pacing and turned to me with a contorted expression. His eyes glittered with unshed tears, and in a tone halfway between a howl and a sob he cried, "*Why is God testing me?*"

I wasn't thinking of this book in that moment. I simply continued to exhort Manuel as best I knew how. Only when I reached home did it occur to me that his question is the one we most often ask when we are suffering. We might phrase it differently, but essentially we all want to know *why* thus and thus is happening.

A couple days after the ER trip, when I felt strong enough to resume writing, I added the section titled "Painful Questions" in the prologue. And as I studied the Book of Job in the ensuing weeks, it struck me that Manuel's question also lies at the core of Job's lament. Baffled by his unexpected and excruciating jolts, Job cries out in much the same manner as Manuel had when he asked, "*Why is God testing me?*"

Job's query is never answered in the biblical narrative, but he receives something infinitely grander: a revelation of God directly from God's mouth. As a bonus, he is blessed with a restoration that puts his former prosperity to shame, and an additional 140 years of life, or "fourteen whole decades," as I put it in the closing stanza of Part VII.

The wish that precedes his greatest confession—"I know my Redeemer lives" (19:25)—is granted as well. Though perhaps posthumously, Job's words are indeed "inscribed in a book," one that gets included in the canon of Scripture and which has comforted innumerable sufferers down through the centuries.

Since my book is primarily a poetic rendition of this biblical text, it cannot address every aspect of suffering. Even so, I hope it will inspire the afflicted to persevere like Job: as his sole New Testament mention states, "You have heard of the perseverance of Job and seen the end intended by the Lord" (James 5:11). In my case, though I am still learning the art of endurance, I believe this book is one such "end intended by the Lord."

NOTE ON PRONUNCIATION

For reasons of rhyme, some line-ending words will have to be pronounced the American way, as in the *Romeo and Juliet* stanza in the prologue where "chance" must rhyme with "romance." Others call for British pronunciation. In Job's first reply to God in Part VII, for example, "immobile" rhymes with "vile." On occasion, a specific accent may also be required internally, within a line, for metrical reasons. Thus, in one of the later stanzas of Part III, "fragmented" is enunciated US style, with the first syllable stressed; and wherever the name Abraham appears in the epilogue, the stress is on the first of *two* syllables ("AB-rhm"). I have tried to keep these instances to a minimum and trust they will not adversely affect the reading experience.

PROLOGUE

The Problem of Pain

How long, O LORD?
How long will You hide Your face from me?
How long shall I take counsel in my soul,
Having sorrow in my heart daily?
How long will my enemy be exalted over me?

—Psalm 13:1-2

Will the Lord cast off forever?
And will He be favorable no more?
Has His mercy ceased forever?
Has His promise failed forevermore?

—Psalm 77:7-8

LORD, why do You cast off my soul?
Why do You hide Your face from me?

—Psalm 88:14

A Universal Bane

There once was a man who suffered
His name many people have heard
For the problem of pain
Is a universal bane
From which no person is buffered.

Not everyone suffers to the extent
Job did, but in any event
We're certain in life
To meet sorrow and strife,
And always without our consent.

Pain is eclectic in form.
You can't say one thing is the norm.
But this is for sure:
We all seek a cure
When sorrows around us do swarm.

Comforts False and True

Not everyone reacts just like Job.
Not everyone tears off their robe.
Their head they don't shave,
For people behave
Differently all over the globe.

Some folks will pick up a drink
When it feels as though they're on the brink,
Or turn to opioid
Their pain to avoid,
And both are addictive, I think.

And then there's the opiate of sex.
While potent and strangely complex,
When selfishly done
Though fleetingly fun
It surely will leave lives in wrecks.

A pleasure that's dubbed retail therapy
Alleviates distresses, but briefly.
For no one can find
True peace of mind
With spree after mad shopping spree.

Quite often our torment to ease
We reach for our favorite munchies.
While eating does comfort,
Our innermost hurt
Is not healed by filling our bellies.

Or we might turn to some sort of fantasy
On phones and computers and TV.
It's common today
To deal with dismay
By escaping this way from reality.

We're trying to deaden the pain
So it doesn't surface again.
However we cope
We all want the hope
That suffering we'll somehow restrain.

We think these escapes are pain experts
And expect them to blot out our hurts,
Lifting the weight
By wiping the slate,
But in fact they are merely false comforts.

False comforts, it's not always obvious,
Soothe for a time, then prove devious.
We're left feeling empty
And still needing plenty
Of solutions that aren't so fugacious.

This means that these means are impermanent,
Which formerly wasn't apparent.
And they are untrue
In promising you
A fix that appears heaven-sent.

The comfort we seek in our suffering
Only God is well able to bring.
His fount is eternal
And can our internal
Wounds give a deep and true healing.

Painful Questions

When we suffer we have this one question
Which we utter with heartfelt emotion.
Our agonized cry
Is *Why, God, oh why?*
Why am I being tried in this fashion?

If we've suffered for years with some wrong
We further inquire *How long?*
We're not very sure
That we can endure
Much more, for we don't feel so strong.

When we ponder the problem in general
As humans it's perfectly natural
To wonder why would
A God who is good
Let evil exist with the moral.

Why do some good people suffer
And the wicked have things far less rougher?
Their journey is smooth
But speaking in truth,
They have nothing worthwhile to offer.

Why must we live with the scars
When wounded through no fault of ours?
For another man's crime
We do the time.
He's let off and we're behind bars.

Why do a few people prosper
Yet millions are poor as a pauper?
Where is the justice
In a system like this?
Disparity is not right and proper.

Why do we wage endless wars
With their grim demonstrations of force?
For certain men's gain
Whole nations retain
A multitude of festering sores.

Why do some people find true love,
A match made in heaven above,
Whereas others yet
Aren't able to get
The partner they pray for and dream of?

Why are some snatched in their prime?
And why does the mourning knell chime
Before to a measure
To taste of life's pleasure
Some children were given the time?

The list could continue but here
Let me just state the premier
Problem of pain:
It seems almost vain
When unmerited, prolonged, and severe.

Pat Answers

There are no easy answers to pain
But you're bound to hear some trite refrain,
Like "Cheer up and smile
For in a wee while
There'll be sunshine instead of the rain."

They'll tell you your blessings to count
For you have a substantial amount,
Like clothing to wear
And food and fresh air.
These basics you must not discount.

They'll remind you that millions of folk
Are sick, all alone, and flat broke.
If your mood is the same
Eventually the name
Of Nick Vujicic they're sure to invoke.

And you may meet that unsympathizer
Who sounds like a mean supervisor.
"Some bad you've done
Has brought all this on.
Sorry, but you should have been wiser."

The kind of insensitive person
Who's unwilling to quietly listen
Interrupts if you moan
With a tale of their own,
Which begins "*That reminds me of when.*"

Others observing your misery
Will suggest that you take up a hobby.
"Go get a pet
Or better yet
Join a dance class or open a charity."

If they possess a more scriptural mind
An apt verse they're certain to find,
Which they duly recite
And because you're polite
You wait in a manner resigned.

Romans 8:28's a favorite.
They'll quote it and later explain it.
"*All* things, you know,
Whether good or not so,
Work *together*, for God has no limit."

Now all of God's Word is terrific
But you need a verse that's specific
To your situation—
A true revelation,
Not a quick fix or something generic.

And now let us go to the place
Where pain first encountered our race.
A consequential thing
We call choice did bring
Distress in terrestrial space.

Of Man's First Disobedience

Suffering we know is our lot
Since a man's disobedience begot
Divine punishment
And swift banishment
From Eden's immaculate spot.

The garden was a heaven on earth.
Whatever God placed there had worth.
Of His paradise
It was a small slice
Till sin brought in sorrow and dearth.

Adam sinned not on his own
And nor was he banished alone.
With him was wife Eve,
Whom the snake did deceive
As he talked in an audible tone.

He asked if indeed God had really
Declared, "You shall not eat of every
Tree of the garden."
And right there in Eden
The woman responded loquaciously.

Instead of just walking away
She spoke to the serpent to say
That God had permitted
All trees but restricted
The one in the middle that lay.

"God told us, 'Do not eat or even
The fruit touch that I have forbidden,
Because when you do
You'll die, each of you.'"
This answer the serpent was given.

That liar then made his reply:
"Assuredly, you shall not die.
God knows when you've eaten
Your eyes then will open;
You'll know good and evil, that's why."

Believing the serpent now she
Did covet the fruit of the tree.
It was a fine sight
And seemed to be right
For eating and gaining sagacity.

Eve ate it and gave Adam some.
He was standing beside as though dumb,
Not thinking to tell
The snake "Go to hell,"
But choosing like Eve to succumb.

When God they did thus disobey
The eyes of both opened and they
Did look down to see
Their own nudity
And initially had nothing to say.

When their senses the two did recover
Each stared at the stark naked lover
Ashamed and afraid
And feeling betrayed,
Sewed fig leaves their bareness to cover.

But God who's all-knowing can see
Our conduct and every activity
Under the sun.
He knew what they'd done
And so to the garden came He.

Out of Eden

It had once been a lovely routine.
Each day God arrived on the scene
For His evening walk
And an intimate talk
With the man and his beautiful queen.

But this time would be very different,
For our parents no longer were innocent.
The visit would be
Without gaiety,
As fear their two hearts did torment.

Today they were hiding in shame,
And when God called out Adam's name
Instantly he
Accused Eve, and she
At the serpent directed the blame.

When God had created humanity
Puppets they weren't meant to be.
He gave them free will
To choose good or ill
And ill they both chose voluntarily.

God's nature is righteous and holy.
Although He's abounding in mercy
He must deal with sin
Or good will not win
And the conscience will always be guilty.

So by the forbidden fruit tree
He gave out each just penalty.
All three of them
The Lord did condemn
For their role in that day's mutiny.

For Adam was cursed the earth's ground.
Thorns everywhere would abound.
By the sweat of his brow
He'd labor from now
Till as dust once again he was found.

For her part in the sad tragedy
Mother Eve would continually be
Filled with desire
For her children's dear sire
And feel terrible pain in delivery.

And as for the serpent, the one
Who had the tempting first done,
On his belly he'd crawl
And best of all
His head would be crushed by her Son!

"Now Adam knows both good and evil,"
The Lord said, "and so lest he will
Of Our tree of life
Eat with his wife,
I'll send him the ground's soil to till."

To cover these two God did slay
An animal and afterwards they,
In garments of skin
Dressed, out of Eden
Made their disconsolate way.

This historical episode we call
Original sin or the fall.
It introduced pain
To the earthly domain,
The incident that started it all.

In Literature as In Life

In literature, just as in life,
We meet sorrow and struggle and strife.
Whatever its plot
A story has got
This note of verismo to strike.

Down through the cultural ages
Poets and playwrights and sages
Have often depicted
How man is afflicted,
In book form as well as on stages.

We find that in every fine tragedy,
Unlike in a lighthearted comedy,
The towering hero
Plunges to zero
From the top rung, without remedy.

Thus when the hand of adversity
Does tap one enjoying prosperity
The fall is so great
It will generate
A catharsis of fear and pure pity.

In Shakespeare the valiant Othello
Was once quite a dignified fellow,
But a lone handkerchief
Does a little mischief
And his temper is anything but mellow.

Distrust in his bosom does spread
As Othello starts losing his head.
Incited by Iago
He picks up a pillow
And soon Desdemona is dead.

It might come across as a parody
When narrated in this kind of poetry,
But watch it in action
And you'll have a reaction
Of fear and dismay and pure pity.

The sad affair of Romeo and Juliet
In Verona's fair city is set.
This tender romance
Does not stand a chance:
He's Montague and she's Capulet.

The households for years have been feuding
When love the scene enters intruding,
But things go awry
And the star-crossed pair die
In a tomb that is bloodstained and brooding.

We may not have seen lovers go
Like Juliet and her Romeo,
But watching the play
Can anyone stay
Unmoved at all by such sweet sorrow?

Hamlet's Soliloquy

Young Hamlet of Denmark the prince
Has lost his dear father, and since
His tongue he must hold
On what he was told,
In soliloquies his grief does evince.

With words his heart Hamlet unpacks
And sorrows with words he attacks.
His most famous question
Evokes a reflection
On life's burdens and many setbacks.

He asks if 'tis nobler in the mind
To suffer when fortune's unkind.
Or do we oppose
Our troubles and woes
When ourselves in their midst we may find?

Self-slaughter, though a measure extreme,
For the sufferer it often does seem
Better instead—
But what if the dead
Go to sleep perchance to dream?

And that is the pause-worthy theorem.
For who can tell what dreams may come
When this mortal coil
And our worldly toil
To the slumber of death do succumb?

So although we without too much effort
Can end our despair and our hurt,
Our lot don't we bear
And deathward don't fare
Though resting in peace is a comfort?

Suicide most don't contemplate,
But doubtless we all can relate
With at least one of those
Heartaches and woes
This soliloquy so well does enumerate.

No wonder it has stood the test
Of time and is rated the best
In all Shakespeare.
Its depth and grandeur
Methinks none will too much protest.

Literature must have the effect
Of stirring each one to reflect
On life and its woes
And the passage that follows,
And *Hamlet* wins in every respect.

Now let us examine the story
That of suffering's an apt allegory,
For Job's tears in the vale
In comparison pale
To the weight of his subsequent glory.

PART I

Job's Jolts

Job 1-3

The LORD said to Satan, "Have you considered My servant Job, that there is none like him on the earth, a blameless and upright man, one who fears God and shuns evil? And still he holds fast to his integrity, although you incited Me against him, to destroy him without cause."

So Satan answered the LORD and said, "Skin for skin! Yes, all that a man has he will give for his life. But stretch out Your hand now, and touch his bone and his flesh, and he will surely curse You to Your face!"

And the LORD said to Satan, "Behold, he is in your hand, but spare his life."

So Satan went out from the presence of the LORD, and struck Job with painful boils from the sole of his foot to the crown of his head. And he took for himself a potsherd with which to scrape himself while he sat in the midst of the ashes.

—Job 2:3-8

In the Land of Uz

JOB 1:1–5, 1:13–22

In the ancient Near East land of Uz
A great man called Job there once was.
Though blameless and upright
He was in God's sight,
He suffered without any cause.

God blessed him with honor and wealth,
Ten children, and also good health.
And then on one day
They were taken away
In disasters all striking by stealth.

Sadly it happened too fast,
From the first crushing blow to the last.
He lost sons and daughters
And servants in slaughters,
Thus his joy went from present to past.

One day in his house all was fine.
Perhaps they had sat down to dine.
They never suspected
Events unexpected
Were brewing as they sipped their wine.

Abruptly a messenger appeared
And this news to Job he delivered:
Sabean marauders
From across Uz's borders
Job's oxen and donkeys had plundered.

In the middle of this man's narration
Another brought new information.
There'd fallen a fire
And the sheepfold entire
Burned up in that one conflagration.

While this man was speaking a third
A fresh punch to poor Job administered.
Chaldeans had invaded,
His camels had raided,
And again many servants were slaughtered.

As Job was digesting each update
A fourth man had news to relate.
And this fellow's story
Was even more gory,
For a strong wind Job's kids did exterminate.

In the oldest one's home all the ten
Were eating and drinking wine when
The aforesaid great gale
Killed female and male.
Job lost at one fell swoop his children.

Hearing this heartrending tale
Job rose with his countenance pale.
His robe he did shred
And shaved clean his head,
Then dropped down with hardly a wail.

"Naked is how I was born
And naked to dust will return.
The gifts the Lord gave
He also can take.
His name I will bless and not spurn."

In all this not once did Job sin.
Though no doubt he must have been in
Profound grief and misery,
Yet he did not query
God or on Him the blame pin.

There surely were times he'd remember
How all of his children would gather
In the home of each son
To feast and have fun
Till the days of festivity were over.

And then Job would rise in the morning
To offer for each a burnt offering.
If God they had cursed
In secret, this worst
Sin did require such a covering.

But now all his children were taken
Along with his sheep and his oxen,
His camels and donkeys,
And most of his flunkeys.
That's how this story does open.

Behind the Scenes in Heaven

JOB 1:6–12, 2:1–6

At this stage we must take a peek
Back of the curtain to seek
How things happened so
To trigger Job's woe
And what made his life downright bleak.

Did Job's aforementioned sad tragedy
Arise without cause and quite senselessly?
Was there not a reason?
Had Job in some season
Stumbled in sin, though unknowingly?

No, it was because the vile devil
Accused Job of not facing ill.
He had divine blessing
And business was booming,
No wonder he trusted God still.

For God had first asked that old serpent:
"Have you been considering My servant?
Like Job there is none
Who evil does shun.
He fears God, is upright, and innocent."

"Does Job fear God simply for nothing?"
Said the one who is always accusing.
"Your hedge him surrounds
And he much abounds,
On all sides enjoying Your blessing.

"His work You make better, not worse.
His possessions aggrandize his purse.
But stretch out Your hand,
Touch his things, and
You to Your face he will curse."

Then God gave the devil permission
To vex Job, with one reservation:
Only his body
Off-limits would be.
The rest had no hedge of protection.

When his great misfortunes began
Job did not, like some lesser man,
Curse God but bless
Him more and not less,
So the devil devised a new plan.

After troubles to Job were first sent,
The angels to God did present
Themselves once again.
In their midst was Satan
And again God did praise Job as excellent.

"No one on earth is as upright.
Though against him you did Me incite,
To hurt him for nothing,
He's blamelessly living
And still his integrity holds tight."

The devil replied, "Skin for skin!
All that a man has he'll trade in
When in his bone
And flesh he does groan.
His body just touch and he'll sin."

The Lord God is not obligated
To do what the devil has stated.
But yet in this case
He did let Job face
Levels of pain we've all hated.

Among the Ashes

JOB 2:7–13, 3:1–2

Large boils most painful did cover
Job's body and his head all over.
No help was his wife
Whom he'd married for life,
But she was a fair-weather lover.

In the ashes when Job she did see
Scraping his sores with some pottery,
"Curse God and die!"
Was her heartless cry.
"Are you still clinging to your integrity?"

"You talk like a mere foolish woman."
More clearly Job could not have spoken,
For in their native tongue
"Foolish" was among
The terms for a dissolute person.

"Shall we take good from God and not bad?
Is good all there is to be had?"
Job in all of this
Sinned not with his lips
Despite being tormented and sad.

Perhaps his wife made no amends
But Job had three well-meaning friends.
The news when they heard
To Uz they all ventured
In hopes of reversing bad trends.

The names of the three amigos are
Eliphaz and Bildad and Zophar.
They wanted to comfort
Their pal in his hurt
And that's why they came from afar.

But when from a distance they spied
His disfigured condition, they cried.
Each one tore his robe
In grief for poor Job
And they sat on the ground by his side.

Each of the three friends had even
Dust on his head toward heaven
Sprinkled to show
They joined in Job's woe.
The days they sat with him were seven.

In this week they said not a thing,
For they noticed how great was his suffering.
To mourn they had come
And so they stayed mum,
Silently with him commiserating.

His mouth then Job opened and spoke,
And with his own words did revoke
The laughter and joy
The gift of a boy
His conception and birth did evoke.

Job's First Lament

JOB 3:3–26

"The day when I chanced to be born
Should not have regarded the morn
But perished at night
Before the first light.
Let God scorn a day so forlorn.

"May the shadow of death now reclaim it!
May a dark cloud my birthday now blanket.
And as for that night,
Let it outright
From the number of months be omit.

"May the same night be childless and barren!
May the night of my very conception
Hear no joyous shout!
Let cursing come out
From those who awaken Leviathan.

"May the stars of its morning be dim.
May its dawning be rayless and grim.
For that day did let
My mother beget
So my life with this sorrow would brim.

"Why did I not die upon birth?
Why living did I appear forth?
And why did I rest
Still on the breast?
I'd be sleeping right now in the earth.

"I'd quietly always be resting
With the counselor and with the king,
And that princely ruler
Who had with silver
And also with gold filled his dwelling.

"Why wasn't I stillborn, a child
Who from the light is undefiled?
In death all the sinful
Cease to be fearful
And the weary are never reviled.

"Prisoners who die are most blest.
The oppressor's voice cannot molest
Their peaceful slumber,
And there's a number
Of slaves who in freedom do rest.

"Why's life lent to someone in misery,
To the anguished soul who does so bitterly
Seek for death's pleasures
Above buried treasures?
The grave he'll encounter rejoicingly.

"Why's light to that man even given
Whose pathway from him does lie hidden?
I'm hemmed in complete
And before I can eat
I sigh for I am with pain stricken.

"My groanings pour out just like liquid.
My eyes cannot shut tight their lid.
The thing that I feared
Has surely appeared
And tranquility from me is hid."

PART II

JOB'S COMFORTERS COMMENCE

JOB 4-10

Then Bildad the Shuhite answered and said:
"How long will you speak these things,
And the words of your mouth be like a strong wind?
Does God subvert judgment?
Or does the Almighty pervert justice?
If your sons have sinned against Him,
He has cast them away for their transgression.
If you would earnestly seek God
And make you supplication to the Almighty,
If you were pure and upright,
Surely now He would awake for you,
And prosper your rightful dwelling place.
Though your beginning was small,
Yet your latter end would increase abundantly."

—Job 8:1-7

Eliphaz Speaks

JOB 4–5

The first of Job's friends to reply
Was Eliphaz from Tema, a guy
Who perhaps did not know
Too much about woe
But mutely he could not sit by.

"If someone tries speaking with you,
Will you grow weary or stew?
But who can contain
His words and remain
Silent when like this you spew?

"No doubt you've instructed so many
And also have strengthened the weary.
The person who stumbled
Or somehow was humbled
You lifted and made much more steady.

"But now you yourself have been hit
With suffering and therefore your spirit
Is troubled and tired.
Aren't you inspired
In reverence and hope to submit?

"Did anyone yet die in their innocence,
Being guiltless of some great offence?
Those who do plow
In sin, that is how
They reap, that has been my experience.

"By the blast of the Lord they will perish.
His anger their lifespan does finish.
The lion sounds fierce
But his prey disappears
And the lioness's young cubs will vanish.

"Now one time it happened quite secretly
A whisper was carried to me
In visions at night.
My bones shook with fright
And the hair did stand up on my body.

"A spirit did glide past my face,
Its appearance I couldn't well trace.
Then it stood still.
It was noiseless until
A voice did the silence replace.

"It spoke saying, 'Tell me who can
As a mortal man be purer than
The Lord up in heaven?
If the Maker will even
His angels not trust, who is man?'

"How much more to blame then are they
Whose dwellings are houses of clay?
They come from the dust
And quickly are crushed,
Like moths that in light's path do stray.

"They're broken in pieces from morning
To evening, with no one regarding.
Their final breath goes
And excellence follows.
They die without wisdom attaining.

"Job, is there someone who will
Answer if you call out still?
For wrath does excise
The man who's unwise
And envy the stupid will kill.

"I have seen the fool taking root,
But abruptly a curse I did execute
Over his dwelling
And now all his offspring
Have enemies in hot pursuit.

"His sons do not have a deliverer.
The people who greatly do hunger
Will eat up his harvest,
Even thorns they'll divest,
And his wealth will be snatched by a robber.

"Affliction comes not from the dust.
The ground does not trouble upthrust,
Yet man's born to woe
As sparks only go
Upward, as always they must.

"But if it were me, I'd appeal
To God and before Him I'd kneel.
To Him would my cause
Be committed because
In marvelous things He does deal.

"He sets those on high who are lowly
And mourners are lifted to safety.
He does send the rain
That waters the plain,
And blocks the intents of the crafty.

"He catches the wise in their cunning,
Bringing their schemes down to nothing.
To them is broad daylight
As dark as the night,
And noontime for them is like evening.

"But the needy are saved from the sword
And the tongue of the strong by the Lord.
The wicked man's hand
Can't bother them, and
Injustice can't utter a word.

"Blest is the one God corrects,
Not the one who His chastening rejects.
For though He may bruise,
His hands He will use
To bind up and heal wounded subjects.

"In your troubles He will liberate you,
And not just in one or in two.
In six ills or seven
And every misfortune
You're certain to have His rescue.

"From cursing tongues you will be hidden
And nor will you fear devastation.
Instead you will smile
And famine revile,
And in war by the sword won't be stricken.

"Of the beasts you will not be afraid,
For a covenant you shall have made
With the stones of the field,
And peace too shall shield
Your tent with its bountiful shade.

"You'll know that your dwelling's secure.
You won't lose what you have in store.
You shall also know
Your family will grow
Like grass that does carpet earth's floor.

"You'll die when you are very old,
Like grain that is ripened to gold.
We've studied this well
It's true, what we tell.
Please hear it, and of it lay hold."

Job Responds

JOB 6–7

"Oh, that my grief could be weighed
And my troubles upon scales were laid!
My suffering would be
Even more weighty
Than sand of the heaviest grade.

"The arrows of God are within.
My spirit imbibes all their toxin.
Because they're arrayed
Against me, I've brayed
Like a donkey who hasn't yet eaten.

"What ox will low over its silage?
Isn't food without salt just like garbage?
Or does the egg white
With flavor delight?
To touch these my soul cannot manage.

"Oh, that I'd have my request,
That God at my anguished behest
Would grant me my plea
And swiftly crush me!
In comfort then always I'd rest.

"If I still had this one consolation
I'd be happy despite my condition.
Let Him not spare.
I've taken good care
To conceal not the Lord's declaration.

"I have come to the end of my rope
And lost the ability to hope.
Does the power of stones
Reside in my bones?
Can anything within help me cope?

"To the person who has been despairing
His friend should show kindness and caring
Although he forsakes,
Because of heartaches,
The fear of the Lord, who's forbearing.

"My brothers now me overlook,
Deceitfully just like a brook
That will in hot weather
Turn snow into vapor
And streams that their trails have forsook.

The brooks, when it's warm, cease to flow.
They arise from their places and go.
The paths of their way
Will change sides and they
Go nowhere and fade away also.

"The caravans arriving from Tema
And travelers from faraway Sheba
Come seeking the stream
But it's vanished in steam,
So they're in a serious dilemma.

"You spot terror and you are afraid.
Have I an appeal to you made
For a bribe or for rescue?
Or else have I asked you
To redeem me from someone's stockade?

"Teach me to see where I've erred.
If you do, I will not say a word.
But all your reproving
Does not prove a thing.
My cries like the wind go unheard.

"To rebuke my words do you intend
And my desperate speeches suspend?
You'd even cast lots
For fatherless tots
And bargain away your own friend.

"Now therefore please look once at me,
For I would never speak to you falsely.
There'll be no injustice
Because I am righteous.
My taste buds detest what's unsavory!

"This life is a time of hard toil
For all those who dwell on earth's soil.
As a servant who earnestly
Wants shade when he's weary
So futility my days does bespoil.

"The moment I lie down I say,
'When will the darkness give way?'
Tossing and turning,
My caked body burning,
I long for the breaking of day.

"My days to the grave quickly hurtle,
Swift as a weaver's fast shuttle.
My life is a breath
Soon ending in death,
Whose rest not a thing can unsettle.

"Before long your eyes will not see me
For I'll very soon cease to be.
As clouds drift away
So those whom we lay
In the grave won't revisit their family.

"And therefore I will not restrain
My tongue or my speeches constrain.
My anguish of spirit
I'll fully exhibit
As I lie on my bed and complain.

"I'll grouse in my bitterness of soul
And surely my couch will console
And offer me comfort
Thus easing my hurt,
For sleep does relief often dole.

"But when You do scare me with dreams
I waken with terrified screams.
Being strangled seems better
Than living forever.
With loathing for life my soul teems.

"A serpent am I of the sea
That You've set a guard over me?
What's man and why
Do You magnify
Him in Your heart so obsessively?

"Why do You relentlessly test
A man without giving him rest?
How long, I pray?
Won't You look away
Till I my saliva ingest?

"What have I done that You set
Me as Your arrow's sole target,
O watcher of men?
To myself I am then
A burden that's filled with disquiet.

"If I've sinned can You not pardon me
And remove far from me my iniquity?
When I lie down in dust
Seek me if You must,
Except I will no longer be."

Bildad Speaks

JOB 8

The next friend to speak was a Shuhite,
Who also felt bad about Job's plight.
But it's rather sad
That this man Bildad
Comes across as a little uptight.

"How long will you blabber like this?
How long like the wind will you hiss?
You think God's unjust?
Or do you not trust
That He won't subvert what is justice?

"If your children committed transgression
And He cast them aside in correction,
Seek God earnestly
And to the Almighty
Humbly present your petition.

"Now if you were upright and pure,
He'd rise up for you, I am sure.
You'd prosper in all.
Though you started out small
You'd end up with more than before.

"Please ask ages past and consider
What their sages did then discover.
We nothing do know,
Our life is a shadow,
But they of their wisdom will utter.

"Can the reed or papyrus plant stand
If it's not planted in a wetland?
While it's yet green
It withers unseen
If there is no water at hand.

"This is the destiny of those
Who forget God and do Him oppose.
Their hope will soon ebb
Like a spider's cobweb,
Which is flimsy and quick to dispose.

"The wicked on his house does lean
But it wobbles and it will careen.
He holds to it fast
But it doesn't last
Even though in the sun he grows green.

"His branches spread out in his garden.
Round rocks are his roots interwoven.
If he is destroyed
The place he enjoyed
Says, 'I never did know this person.'

"Others take over his berth,
For this is the way on the earth.
God will not reject
The one who's correct
But the wicked will feel only dearth.

"Your mouth He will fill up with laughing
And your lips will pour forth rejoicing.
Those hating your name
Will wear robes of shame
And their tents will be flattened to nothing."

Job Responds

JOB 9–10

"Yes, I'm aware this is normal,
But how can a man who is mortal
Claim righteous to be
Before the Almighty,
Whom no one can treat as an equal?

"God's wise and abounding in power
And who can resist Him and prosper?
The mountains He levels
And earth He unsettles
So its pillars do tremble in terror.

"The sun He commands and it harkens;
The starry host likewise He darkens.
The waves He does tread
And alone He has spread
Above earth the highest of heavens.

"The Bear and Orion and Pleiades
He created, and more beside these.
If He passes by
I can't if I try
See Him, for my eye naught perceives.

"If God takes away, tell me who
Can ask, 'What is this that You do?'
He will not withdraw
His wrath when it's raw.
The friends of the proud know this too.

"Then can I with my Judge dispute?
What words would I even recruit?
For though I am innocent
I would be content
To beg mercy and God not refute.

"If I called and He did answer me
I wouldn't believe it was He.
I'm hurt without cause.
I can't even pause
For breath as my soul is so heavy.

"If justice is my last resort
Then who'll grant me my day in court?
Although I am blameless
My own mouth in witness
Will utter a twisted report.

"I'm blameless but yet I despise
My own self, because in God's eyes
The good and the wicked
Are equally wretched.
Would I suffer thus otherwise?

"If the scourge renders one a fatality
He'll mock their sad plight and calamity.
He's covered the faces
Of all of the judges.
Earth's rulers are men of iniquity.

"My days can outrun any sprinter,
Darting through summer and winter
As an eagle does swoop
Its prey to fast scoop
Or a ship swiftly skims over water.

"If I say, 'I will cease to complain
And a smile on my countenance feign,'
You still will see me
As one who is guilty.
Why then do I labor in vain?

"If I wash myself with snowy water
And soap on my hands if I splatter,
Yet into the pit
You'll plunge me and it
Will make my own garments my hater.

"But He's not a man as am I,
Or we'd go to court by and by.
And no mediator
Does stand in the center
Of us, so we'll both testify.

"His rod let Him take far away from me
So I wouldn't fear Him so terribly.
Only then would I speak
And not be so meek,
But alas, that's not so in reality.

"My soul loathes my very existence,
And so I'll complain with persistence.
To God I'll say bitterly:
Do not oppose me
Or condemn me with no shred of evidence.

"Does it seem good to You to oppress
Me, but not evil redress?
Do Your eyes like man's
At sin simply glance
But closely watch me nonetheless?

"Are Your days like the days of a man
That You for iniquity scan?
With guilt I don't drip
And yet from Your grip
To free me there's no one who can.

"The hands of my Maker have fashioned me,
An intricate being in unity.
Remember, I pray,
You made me like clay.
Like cheese You did curdle my body.

"You clothed me with skin and with flesh,
My sinews with bones did enmesh.
You granted to me
Life in Your mercy
And daily preserve me afresh.

"These things You have hid in Your heart.
You knew all of it from the start.
If I lift high my crown
You will hunt me down
Like a lion that will tear me apart.

"If I sin You will not just acquit
My guilt, but will credit me with it.
Were I not to blame
In the least bit, yet shame
And disgrace I would somehow exhibit.

"You display Your extraordinary power
Against me, Your witnesses glower
In my direction,
And Your vexation
Like an army is making me cower.

"Then why did You let me come forth?
Oh, that I'd perished at birth
And gone from the womb
Straight to the tomb!
I wish I had not seen this earth!

"My days—are they not but a few?
Then leave me to briefly accrue
Some joy before
My life is no more
And I depart for my ultimate venue.

"This country to which I shall go
Is the region of darkness and shadow.
It possesses no order
Or life whatsoever.
Even light there does somberly glow."

PART III

JOB'S COMFORTERS CONTINUE

JOB 11-17

Then Zophar the Naamathite answered and said:
"Should not the multitude of words be answered?
And should a man full of talk be vindicated?
Should your empty talk make men hold their peace?
And when you mock, should no one rebuke you?
For you have said,
'My doctrine is pure
And I am clean in your eyes.'
But oh, that God would speak,
And open His lips against you,
That He would show you the secrets of wisdom!
For they would double your prudence.
Know therefore that God exacts from you
Less than your iniquity deserves."

—Job 11:1-6

Zophar Speaks

JOB 11

Then the Naamathite comforter, Zophar,
Wordlessly who'd listened so far,
Began to upbraid
Job for that tirade,
Which to him seemed a bit too bizarre.

"Should we let this insane teeming flow
Of verbosity unanswered go?
Do we hold our peace
As Job spews out these
Speeches both scornful and hollow?

"Your doctrine you claim is pristine
And reckon yourself to be clean.
Oh, that the Lord
Would but say a word
And rebuke you for venting your spleen!

"If He showed you the secrets of wisdom
You would doubly prudent become.
Of this thing be sure
That God exacts for
Your guilt so much less than is custom.

"Can you search out His depths or His limits?
You know they surpass the high summits
Of heaven and patrol
Way deeper than Sheol,
Past seas and the earth's very cubits.

"His judgment of us can't be hindered.
Men's wickedness He has considered.
An ignorant dolt
Is wise when the colt
Of a donkey as man is delivered.

"If ever your heart you'd prepare
And reach out in genuine prayer,
If you just cast off sin
And don't let it in
Your tents, you would not have a care.

"You'd lift up your face unabashedly
And steadfast you'd certainly be.
Your woes you'd forget;
This trouble and fret
Would become nothing more than a memory.

"Your life would be shining as bright
As noonday, yes, even at night.
You would be secure
Your hope would be sure.
In safety you would sleep at night.

"You'd lie down without any terror
And multitudes would court your favor.
But as for the wicked
Their end is so wretched!
Their hope will die when life is over."

Job Responds

JOB 12–14

"No doubt all you men are so wise
That wisdom in you lives and dies!
But I can think too;
I'm not less than you.
Who does not such stuff realize?

"I'm one whom his own friends do mock!
When I on God's front door did knock
He did answer me.
Though blameless I be
I'm scoffed at like some laughingstock.

"A lamp is despised in the mind
Of him who with tears isn't blind.
Instead it is ready
For him who's unsteady,
To whom life has been quite unkind.

"The dwellings of robbers are prosperous.
The people who can be preposterous
Enough to provoke
The Lord don't invoke
Troubles that may be disastrous.

"Just ask any land or sea creature.
A bird even could be your teacher.
They'll all say it is
God who did this.
Who does not know this fact in nature?

"All living things' life He does hold.
Man's breath by His hand is controlled.
The mouth and the ear
Do taste and do hear
And wisdom resides with the old.

"With God are true wisdom and might.
His counsel is weighty, not light.
What things He does tear
No man can repair.
There's none who His judgments can fight.

"If God throws a man into jail
Nobody can post that man's bail.
If He stops the rain,
The rain will refrain
Till He tips the celestial pail.

"The deceived and deceiver are His.
He even makes fools of the judges.
He reduces fierce kings
To meek underlings
And leads away princes as captives.

"He hushes the trusted advisers
And cuts off the insight of elders.
He shames the nobility
And weakens the mighty.
Things hid in the dark He uncovers.

"He destroys or else raises to greatness
The nations and takes away brightness
From all of their chiefs.
They experience griefs
As they wander about in the wilderness.

They grope in the dark without light,
Staggering from left to right
Like a drunkard or sot.
This is the lot
Of those God has stripped of their might.

"All this I see and believe in.
I've heard and discerned this much, even.
The same things that you
Comprehend I do too,
But with *God* I'm desiring to reason.

"What forgers of lies you all are,
Most worthless physicians by far!
If silent you'd be
Your wisdom I'd see.
My pleadings now do not debar.

"For God will you wickedly speak?
But what if it's *you* He would seek?
If you are not pure
He'll rebuke you for sure
And the dread of Him will make you weak.

"For God will you argue today
And sly partiality display?
Your minds possess stashes
Of proverbs of ashes.
Your defenses are defenses of clay.

"Be silent and do hold your peace
And let me have time to speak, please,
Then let come what may!
Why do I this way
Take perilous risks such as these?

"Now this is what I want to say:
Although He may slay me someday
Yet Him will I trust.
Endure what I must,
Before Him I'll champion my way.

"This is my firm resolution,
And He'll also be my salvation.
Though no hypocrite
Could ever say it,
Please listen to my declaration.

"My case I've prepared and made airtight
And am certain that I shall be proved right.
If I'm silent now
I'll perish somehow.
So who's he who with me will fight?

"And thus having stated my case
I only solicit God's grace.
I'm asking that You
These two things do,
So from You I won't hide my face.

"Please move Your hand from me much farther
And let me not feel so much terror.
Then summon, and I
Will surely reply,
Or else I can be the first speaker.

"How vast is my sin and iniquity
That You regard me with enmity?
And will You so frighten
A dry leaf that's driven
Around and about without pity?

"My youthful sins You make me reap
And both feet in stocks You do keep.
My ways You inspect,
My soles You subject
To limits, as they do for sheep.

"Men decay like a thing that is rotten
Or a garment that now is moth-eaten.
We breathe our last
And our life is past.
Like vapor or mist we're forgotten.

"Man who of woman is born
Has few days, and all of them careworn.
He flees like a shadow.
Like a flower in the meadow
He fades away fast and forlorn.

"And such a frail one do You judge?
Can pureness be got from a smudge
Or any dark blot?
Of course it cannot!
Why then do You bear me a grudge?

"You've set and determined a plan
For the tenure of every lifespan.
So please look away
That we mortals may
End like a tired hired man.

"There's hope for a freshly felled tree,
Dead though its stump seems to be.
At the fragrance of moisture
As happens in nature
New branches will sprout forth eventually.

"But a dead man is buried forever.
Till the heavens dissolve he will never
From death's sleep arise.
Below ground he lies,
Vanished like some dried-up river.

"Oh, that You'd hide me in the grave
Till Your anger is past, and will save
For me a set date!
Then I will wait
For the change and relief that I crave.

"Shall a man who expires live again?
You'll call and I will not refrain
From making reply,
Thus a record of my
Iniquity You won't maintain.

"The work of Your hands You desire.
My sin and my steps in the mire
In a bag that is sealed
All will be concealed,
For You've covered up each one entire.

"As mountains collapse and then crumble
And torrents on stones swiftly tumble,
Eroding as they rush,
So You too can crush
Man's hope, whether lofty or humble.

"You prevail over man and he dies.
His sons' future lows and their highs
He'll never perceive.
He only can grieve
While a frame of flesh he occupies."

Eliphaz Speaks

"Job, you are full of hot air.
The person who's wise wouldn't dare
This fashion to argue.
Your words have no value.
You discard fear of God and true prayer.

"Your speeches arise from iniquity.
Such rhetoric is that of the crafty.
Your own tongue, not mine,
Is the real telltale sign,
Testifying that you are guilty.

"Are you the first person born ever?
Does God counsel secretly whisper
In your ear alone?
Is all wisdom known
Only by you and no other?

"Or did you appear before hills?
And what is the knowledge that fills
Your head and not ours?
Do we lack your powers?
Are we wanting in your special skills?

"The gray-haired and aged have spoken.
Are the sweet consolations of heaven
Too slight for you?
The statements you spew
Rancor towards God do betoken.

"Those who have counseled you gently
In lifespan and age have seniority
Over your father.
Yet you would rather
Glower and glare at us angrily.

"Humans, each one, are blameworthy.
Saints even are not trustworthy.
If the loftiest skies
Aren't pure in God's eyes
What's man, who is morally filthy?

"Whatever I've seen I'll declare,
What wise men have also laid bare
And haven't kept hidden.
Their fathers were given
The land where no foreigners fare.

"The wicked man writhes in his pain
Not knowing how many remain
Of his allotted years.
And he always fears
In riches one day he'll be slain.

"He believes that he will not come back
From darkness that's thick and pitch black.
A sword is awaiting
For him, like a king
Who is armed and prepared for attack.

"He wanders in search of his bread
Expecting that dark day ahead.
Trouble and anguish
His confidence vanquish,
And his heart's always bursting with dread.

"The Almighty this man has defied
And stubborn resistance applied.
Dwelling in opulence
And every indulgence,
His waist has with fatness grown wide.

"He resides in a desolate city,
Where houses lie vacant and empty.
Each one is destined
To fully be ruined
And he'll surely come into poverty.

"His property will not continue
And when his existence is through,
With one final breath
He will get in death
The futile reward he is due.

"His branches will not remain green.
In his lifetime this thing will be seen.
His blossoms will drop
And wildfire will stop
The tents in which trouble does preen.

"He ran against God with his shield
So emptiness his life will yield.
It's true the assembly
Of hypocrites will be
Like a barren, untillable field."

Job Responds

JOB 16–17

"What miserable comforters you are!
Your words have been vacuous so far.
I've heard such things too,
So what provokes you
That you answer with speeches that scar?

"Were you in the place of my soul
I too could send down a shoal
Of statements your way,
But all that I'd say
Would strengthen and bless and console.

"I speak but I get no relief
And silence won't lessen my grief.
It's wearing me out.
My frailty, no doubt,
Against me is witness-in-chief.

"God tears me apart in His fury,
Gnashing at me like an enemy.
And as for my friends,
Their censure descends
As a slap on the face, very scornfully.

"He's given me up to the godless
And shattered my peace and my easiness.
He took me by the neck
And shook me like a speck
Of dust into a fragmented mess.

"His archers about me surround
And in them no pity is found.
My heart too He stabs
With arrow-like jabs
And then pours my blood on the ground.

"With wound upon wound He does break me
And runs like a warrior who's mighty.
A sackcloth I've sewn
Over my skin and bone
To signify my grim calamity.

"My head I have laid in the dust.
My face is the color of rust
From constantly crying.
I feel like I'm dying
Though my prayer's pure and blameless, I trust.

"O earth, do not cover my blood
And don't at my wailing fling mud!
Though my friends vilify,
To my witness on high
In tears my eyes pour out their flood.

"Oh, that a person might plead
For a man with the Lord God indeed
As he does for a friend!
For when my years end
On the way of no return I'll proceed.

"My lifespan is nearly extinguished.
The grave is now ready and furnished.
Aren't mockers with me?
And can't my eye see
The reproofs they have hostilely brandished?

"Now put down for me please a pledge.
I must have a guarantor's hedge.
Don't let them prevail!
The children will fail
Of those who do falsely allege.

"Alas, He has made me a maxim,
Everyone's face-spitting victim.
Where once I had praise
Now only malaise,
And sorrow has made my eye dim.

"The upright are shocked when they see it
And rise up against the vile hypocrite.
Yet will the righteous
Stick to his compass,
Being stronger and having more grit.

"Please try once again, all you guys,
For none among you is that wise.
My days are now past.
My plans are down cast,
The things that my heart did devise.

"The night they transform into day
And when it is dark they will say,
'The light is quite near.'
The grave, I do fear,
Is the house where I always will stay.

"If I called death's corruption my father
And the maggots my sister and mother,
What then is my hope
But a gossamer rope?
Won't we rest in the earth's dust together?"

PART IV

Job's Comforters Conclude

Job 18-25

Then Eliphaz the Temanite answered and said:
"Can a man be profitable to God,
Though he who is wise may be profitable to himself?
Is it any pleasure to the Almighty that you are righteous?
Or is it gain to Him that you make your ways blameless?
Is it because of your fear of Him that He corrects you,
And enters into judgment with you?
Is not your wickedness great,
And your iniquity without end?"

—Job 22:1-5

Bildad Speaks

A new phase of Job's long debate
Now opens, and sad to relate,
Not one of the friends
Tried making amends
But continued poor Job to berate.

"How long will you keep up this prattle?
Your soul with resentment does rattle.
Get wiser and then
We'll talk like grown men.
You think we're as stupid as cattle?

"The light of the wicked does end.
The flame of his fire will descend
To a vanishing spark
Till his tent becomes dark,
And his vigor too far won't extend.

"He's cast in a net by his feet.
A snare he is certain to meet.
His heel it will grip
And cause him to trip.
For him a trap's laid in the street.

"Terrors attack on each side
And fear makes him run far and wide.
He loses his strength
And sickness at length
Will feast on his limbs and his hide.

"Removed from the place of his dwelling,
He's brought to the terrifying king.
When brimstone uproots
His tent and his offshoots
The memory of him fades to nothing.

"He's driven from light into darkness,
Chased from the world with all promptness.
He has no renown
And in his hometown
The houses are known by their emptiness.

"This person will die in obscurity
Without any son or posterity.
In both east and west
They will be distressed
When the godless man faces adversity."

Job Responds

"How long will you verbally maim
My soul thus with no sense of shame?
Your reproaches I've heard.
If indeed I have erred
I'll accept I am worthy of blame.

"You think of yourselves as superior
And argue against my behavior.
But know that the net
It's God who has set
Around and about my exterior.

"If I cry out I'm surely not heard
And justice to me isn't rendered.
He's fenced up my way
And taken away
The crown that had once my head covered.

"He's uprooted my hope like a tree
And kindled His anger against me.
His forces He sent
To encircle my tent,
Treating me like I'm an enemy.

"My kinfolk He's moved very far,
My acquaintances also does bar
From paying me a visit.
My close friends have split.
I'm forgotten like something bizarre.

"They loathe me who dwell in my house.
When I call out my servants won't rouse
To meet just one need.
I'm offensive indeed
To my brothers as well as my spouse.

"Even youngsters do me much despise.
Against me they speak when I rise.
Abhorred and alone
I'm but skin and bone,
Having narrowly escaped my demise.

"Have pity on me, friends, have pity,
For the Lord's hand severely has struck me!
Why do you oppress
As He does, unless
You've not had enough of my misery?

"Oh, that my words were now written,
Inscribed on a rock with a pen!
In a book or a scroll
With lead or with coal
I wish they were hewn and engraven!

"For I know my Redeemer's alive
And shall on the last day arrive
To stand on earth's dust,
And I fully trust
That to see Him from death I'll revive.

"My skin will by then be decayed
But before me He will be displayed,
And when I arise
I'll see with my eyes.
I yearn, and I won't be dismayed!

"If you choose to persecute me
And charge me with guilt and iniquity,
For yourselves be afraid
As you'll be repaid.
God's judgment's a sure guarantee."

Zophar Speaks

JOB 20

"My disquieting, anxious thoughts, therefore,
Cause me to reply only once more.
I have heard the insult
And as a result
I can't your reproaches ignore.

"This fact do you not know with certainty
That down through humanity's history
Momentary is
The hypocrite's bliss
And brief is the wrongdoer's victory?

"Though his pride reaches up to the sky
And his head also mounts very high
He'll perish forever
Being seen again never.
Like a dream that is vanished he'll fly.

"The eye that beheld this man once
Will not again at his face glance.
His children will seek
The help of the meek
When in dust he does end his existence.

"His sin's like a tasty confection
Retained under his tongue's protection.
In it he does wallow
Like sweets he won't swallow
But cherishes with fond affection.

"Yet his food does turn sour in the stomach
And in him sin's poison wreaks havoc.
His ill-gotten riches
By vomit he ditches
And the venom of cobras he'll suck.

"By the viper's bite will he be slayed.
He won't see the flowing cascade
Of honey and cream
In river or stream
But return all the wealth that he made.

"He won't enjoy his business profits
For the poor he has tortured to bits.
He has seized the houses
Not rightfully his—
And violently, as done by bandits.

"His craving is not satisfied,
Therefore it will be denied.
His food will not last,
His health will fade fast,
And distress will be close by his side.

"He will feel the full force of misery.
While eating he will face the fury
Of the anger of God.
He'll flee from the sword
But be pierced through by bronze archery.

"Its tip will come out of his gall,
And for all his treasures a pall
Pitch black is reserved.
He won't be preserved
When fire on his dwelling does fall.

"The heavens will lay bare his sin.
His possessions are destined for ruin.
They will flow away
On God's chosen day,
And thus will God bring discipline."

Job Responds

"My speech you must hear very carefully
And let this your consolation be.
When I am done talking
You may go on mocking,
But please until then bear with me.

"If my grouse is against any mortal
Will not my impatience be normal?
But look at my state
And cease to berate.
I myself dread to think on my trouble!

"So why do the wicked grow old,
Getting mighty in power untold?
Their offspring arise
In front of their eyes
And disaster steers clear of their threshold.

"They don't face God's fury on average.
Their cows calve without one miscarriage.
To the sounding of music
Their kids dance and frolic,
And sing songs with joy and glad visage.

"Transgressors their days spend quite gainfully
Then die in a trice, and not painfully.
Although they will say
To God, 'Go away!
Your laws we consider disdainfully.

"'Who's God that we ought to serve Him?
Does prayer to Him with profit brim?'
Yet all they command
Is not in their hand.
Their counsel will not near me swim.

"How oft is their candle put out?
Does trouble on them often sprout
To strike them with woes?
They're like straw that blows
And chaff that the wind whisks about.

"They say, 'God does store our iniquity,
Reserving it for our posterity.'
Well, let God repay
This man so he may
With his eyes gaze upon his calamity.

"Of the anger of God let him drink.
For he's not required to think
Of the son or the daughter
Who will follow after
When his lifespan is halved and does shrink.

"Can anyone teach the Judge knowledge?
When one person reaches his passage
His pails overflow.
His bones possess marrow,
For in life he had every advantage.

"Another will perish in lowliness,
His poor soul abounding in bitterness.
But both men indeed
Will die and will feed
Earth's worms as they lie in death's darkness.

"Behold, I can read your thoughts well,
Your schemes I am able to smell.
You ask, 'Where's the palace?'
And want to know where is
The place in which wrongdoers dwell.

"Have you never asked people who travel?
Their accounts aren't just fanciful drivel.
On God's day of doom
His fury will fume
On the sinful and cause men to marvel.

"Who condemns the vile man to his face?
And who all his actions repays?
But yet his dead body
They'll properly bury
And a guard at his tomb they will place.

"His grave is as deep as a valley
And sweet will its clods to him be.
All people will die.
How then do you try
To comfort with words that are empty?"

Eliphaz Speaks

"Can a person to God be of benefit,
Though a wise man may bring himself profit?
Is God at all joyous
Because you are pious?
Does your virtue affect Him one whit?

"Does He chide you because of your reverence
And against you for that have a grievance?
Job, isn't your wickedness
Immense, even limitless?
You stripped the poor naked, for instance.

"You did not give drink to the weary
And withheld your own bread from the hungry.
The widow and fatherless
You sent away helpless
But welcomed the noble and mighty.

"Therefore around you are snares
And abrupt trepidation now scares.
The darkness surrounds you.
It's shrouding the view
So you drown in a flood tide of cares.

"Isn't God in the summit of heaven,
Far above all the highest stars, even?
You say, 'Does God know
What goes on below?
Through thick clouds the world can He govern?'

"Will you walk where the sinful have trod,
Those swept away by a swift flood
Before it was time
Because of their crime?
'Depart from us!' said they to God.

"What could the Almighty One do?
And yet He was kind enough to
Fill up their dwellings
With plenty of fine things,
Of which they weren't worthy, it's true.

"The advice of the vile isn't near me.
Their end righteous people will see.
'Our foes have all perished
And wildfire has finished
What remains,' they will say with great glee.

"Submit now to God, be at peace,
Then favor will find you, and please
Receive His instruction.
For your life's construction
Expel from your tent your iniquities.

"Then will the gold that you own
Be merely a riverbed stone.
Your gold and your silver
Will be your Creator.
You'll delight in the Almighty alone.

"To Him you will make every prayer.
You'll pay the vows you once did swear.
The thing you decree
Will come to you surely,
And light on your ways will then flare.

"To him who is downcast you'll say,
'Promotion is coming your way!'
That one will be saved.
And yes, the depraved
Will be rescued because you did pray."

Job Responds

"My complaint still possesses its bitterness.
My hand from my groaning is listless.
Oh, that my mind
Knew where to find
God's seat of His mercy and goodness!

"My case then to Him I'd present.
My mouth I would fill up with argument.
His reply I'd receive.
He'd not, I believe,
Oppose me though He is omnipotent.

"No, but instead He would notice
Me, for that is where the righteous
Can reason and plead,
And I'm sure indeed
That forever I would obtain justice.

"Yet He's not there when I go forward.
I can't see Him when I go backward.
To the left or the right
He's nowhere in sight
And my vision of Him now is blurred.

"But He knows the way that I hold
And when He has tried me, as gold
Of dross that is purged
I shall have emerged.
My foot to His paths has kept hold.

"I've followed His steps very closely.
His commandment I've heeded completely.
Whatever He's said
I've loved more than bread
And the portion of food I eat daily.

"But God is unique, and say who
Can change Him, for He'll always do
All that He wishes.
What's appointed He finishes,
For me and in other things too.

"Therefore I fear my God's presence.
I'm afraid and I've lost my old confidence
Because I didn't die
Before harm came nigh,
And nor did He cover my countenance.

"Since the season for every activity
Isn't hidden from God the Almighty,
Why don't His allies
Behold with their eyes
The days when He judges the guilty?

"The wicked move landmarks and boundaries
And violently others' flocks seize.
With donkeys and oxen
Of the widow and orphan
They callously do as they please.

"The needy ones they push aside,
Forcing the poor folks to hide
In deserts and scour
For scraps to devour,
So the wasteland their food does provide.

"They gather their fodder in fields
And glean what the rich vineyard yields.
They haven't got clothing
To give them some cloaking.
No sack from the cold night them shields.

"Lacking the shelter of bowers
They're soaked to the skin by the showers.
They huddle around
A rock or a mound
And thus pass the long rain-lashed hours.

"The villain will snatch from the breast
The babe, and the needy divest
Of garment and grain.
The poor must refrain
From drinking the wine they have pressed.

"The dying ones groan in the city.
The souls of the wounded for pity
Do cry out, and yet
The wicked don't get
Charged by the Lord with iniquity.

"They freely rebel against light,
Shunning the paths that are right.
At dawn will the murderer
Slay the poor laborer,
And the thief does his stealing at night.

"Dusk is the time the adulterer
Conceals his real face with a cover.
Much evil is done
In the dark, for the sun
Fills sinners with panic and terror.

"In their view the morning is equal
To the shadow of death; it's a signal
That someone may see
Their unmasked identity,
An event they're afraid could prove fatal.

"Their vineyards are under a curse
And no one that way does traverse.
As streams of snow cave
To the heat so the grave
Snaps up those who've been perverse.

"The worm on that man's corpse should feed,
And his mother herself should indeed
Forget he once was.
I say this because
He oppressed women who were in need.

"The strong man God takes with His power.
Security on some He does shower.
On it they rely
But God with His eye
Observes how they spend every hour.

"For a while they're exalted then die,
Brought low though were formerly high.
If this isn't so
Then who here will show
My speech is worth naught and I lie?"

Bildad Speaks

"To God belong awe and dominion.
He sovereignly rules over heaven.
Can anyone count
His armies' amount?
On whom has His light not arisen?

"How then can a mortal man be
Good before God the Almighty?
Or how can the person
Who's born of a woman
Claim to possess any purity?

"If the moon does not shine forth its light
And the stars are not pure in His sight,
How then can a man
Who's little more than
A worm and a maggot be upright?"

PART V

JOB'S LAST LAMENT

JOB 26-31

Job further continued his discourse, and said:
"Oh, that I were as in months past,
As in the days when God watched over me;
When His lamp shone upon my head,
And when by His light I walked through darkness;
Just as I was in the days of my prime,
When the friendly counsel of God was over my tent;
When the Almighty was yet with me,
When my children were around me;
When my steps were bathed with cream,
And the rock poured out rivers of oil for me!"

—Job 29:1-6

Faint Are the Whispers

JOB 26

When Bildad did call man a maggot
In Job it unfastened a spigot,
For a lengthy reply
He did speechify
As he ranted like some rankled zealot.

"Have you ever helped him who is powerless
Or saved one who's brimming with weakness?
Did you counsel the unwise
Or anyone advise?
To whom have you made all your speeches?

"The dead agitate in deep anguish
And Sheol before God does languish.
He stretches the north
And hangs up the earth
On nothing, yet it doesn't vanish.

"In thick clouds He binds up the waters
And the face of His throne room He covers.
He drew a horizon,
A circle upon
The place where the day night encounters.

"The pillars of heaven do tremble
With shock when His reprimands rumble.
He stirs up the sea
With force and authority,
And the storm can with ease disassemble.

"The heavens His Spirit has decked.
The serpent His hand does dissect.
And this is a fraction
Of His work and His action—
How faint are the whispers we detect!

What Is the Hope of the Hypocrite?

JOB 27

"As God lives, who's taken my justice
And filled up my soul with such bitterness,
While breath I have got
My mouth's tongue will not
Tell falsehoods or speak any wickedness.

"Till death I'll maintain my integrity
And cling to my righteousness tightly.
My heart won't chastise
But those who do rise
Against me, like the wicked shall be.

"For what is the hope of the hypocrite
When God takes his breath and his spirit?
Will God hear his call
When troubles befall?
Is delight in the Almighty his habit?

"I'll teach you about His great might
And into His ways offer insight.
I'm sure all of you
Have noticed it too.
Why then are you so impolite?

"This is what God gives the wicked
And thus are the ruthless rewarded:
If he has more children
They'll starve in a famine
Or will be by the sword decimated.

"His widow won't mourn and won't cry
Or grieve for the offspring who die.
Though raiment and silver
He has in large number,
To the guiltless it goes by and by.

"His house like the web of a spider
Is merely a temporary shelter.
He lies down in wealth
But loses his health
And soon he's existing no longer.

"By terrors is he overtaken.
His life by a tempest is stolen.
An eastern wind blows
And away this man goes!
Like dust from his place he is driven.

"The east wind at him hurls unsparingly.
He flees from its power despairingly.
Those who observe this
Will clap and will hiss.
With jeering they'll shoo him uncaringly.

Where Can Wisdom Be Found?

JOB 28

"Surely a mine there's for silver,
And gold also has a refiner.
From earth's dust is iron
Assiduously taken,
And by heat ore is smelted for copper.

"Man's light puts an ending to darkness
As he searches in every dim recess.
He opens a shaft
And swings fore and aft
In a far-off remote wilderness.

"The earth underneath is as fire.
Its stones are the sources of sapphire,
And gold it contains.
These secret domains
No lion or bird can admire.

"When man on the flint puts his hand
The bases on which mountains stand
Will topple and show
Gems hidden below,
And he dams up each watery strand.

"Treasures exist underground
But oh, where can wisdom be found?
Man knows not its worth.
It's nowhere on earth,
And the seas do not with it abound.

"It cannot be purchased with gold
And silver for it can't be sold.
There's no precious stone
Or jewelry we own
To be traded so wisdom we'll hold.

"Wisdom is worth more than rubies.
Corals, although they are beauties,
And the best kind of topaz
That Ethiopia has
By contrast are beggarly trumperies.

"Then where does this wisdom reside?
From the living it does seem to hide,
And all Death can offer
Is hearsay and rumor,
For wisdom has only one guide.

"The Lord knows where wisdom does dwell.
The heavens and earth He sees well.
He gave wind a weight
And did regulate
How high ocean waters would swell.

"When God for the rain made a law
And the thunderbolt's pathway did draw,
When He had declared it
As He had prepared it,
Wisdom was in all that He saw.

"And then God to man said this word:
'Behold, it's the fear of the Lord
That truly is wisdom,
And parting ways from
Sin is discernment considered.'

Those Were the Days

"Oh, to be back in the past,
When the hand of God did hold me fast!
His candle burned bright
And I walked by His light,
For His counsel was friendly and vast.

"Those were the days the Almighty
And my children were still around me,
When my footsteps were buttered
And rocks even spluttered
Rivers of rich oil aplenty!

"To the gate of the city I'd fare
And be seated in our public square.
The young men withdrew
And the elderly crew
Arose when they spotted me there.

"The rulers from talking refrained
And the nobles same manner abstained
From uttering speech.
I was blessed by each.
Their approval of me never waned.

"Because the poor man I'd deliver,
And those who did not have a helper.
The one who was passing
Did give me his blessing
And my aid made the widow much happier.

"My justice I wore like a robe.
A father to the poor was your Job.
To the blind I was eyes,
The lame I helped rise,
And the stranger's case with care did probe.

"I shattered the fangs of the wicked.
'I'll die in my own nest,' I said.
'My days are like sand,
My bow's in my hand,
And my root to the waters does spread.'

"The people would wait for my counsel.
My speeches upon them would settle
As sweetly as dew.
Quietly they'd chew
On my talk like a savory morsel.

"They drank up my words like the rain.
I'd tease them at times, but in vain.
They saw me as chief,
A consoler of grief,
And king-like o'er them I did reign.

Ashes and Dust

"But now at me youngsters do mock
Whose fathers to place with my flock
I did not see fit.
For what is the profit
Of one who with old age does rock?

"These wretches from famine are gaunt.
They flee to the wasteland from want.
The mallow they pluck
And tree roots do suck
For food in the deserts they haunt.

"Like robbers, they were without pity
Expelled from the populous city.
In caverns they settled,
Beneath nettles nestled,
Whose dads were the dregs of society.

"And now I'm their mean taunting song.
Their abhorrence of me is so strong
They spit in my face.
God's allowed my disgrace
So they brazenly do me much wrong.

"At my right hand the rabble arises,
At my feet springing nasty surprises.
My movements they bar,
My paths also mar.
I see sorrows in all shapes and sizes.

"They come at me like a large crowd
Of waves that reach high and are loud.
They've chased off my dignity,
And all my prosperity
Has passed like a wind-driven cloud.

"My soul is worn out by my plight.
My bones pierce within me at night.
The days of affliction
Have taken possession
And my pain's end is nowhere in sight.

"Disease does my skin quite disfigure.
It chokes like my overcoat's collar.
As ashes and dust
I've become and am thrust
By God in the mud-splattered mire.

"I cry but You don't answer me.
When I stand up You just glance aloofly.
To me You've become
Both cruel and fearsome.
You oppose me with power and potency.

"You toss me about in the wind.
My success You have utterly ruined.
You will let me die.
To the grave's house will I
Soon go, as each person is destined.

"Surely from a rubble-piled heap
His hand the Almighty would keep?
Did not my soul mourn
For the poor and forlorn?
For those in distress didn't I weep?

"But evil my way came, not good,
And darkness for light when I looked.
My heart is in turmoil,
In unrest does roil
As affliction in my way has stood.

"I'm blackened but not by the sun.
This tanning my grieving has done.
When in the assembly
I stand up and humbly
Holler for help, I get none.

"To jackals I now am a brother.
My skin becomes black and a fever
Does burn in my bones.
My instruments' tones
Are tuned to the tones of the mourner.

Thistles and Weeds

JOB 31

"A covenant I've made with my eyes
Young maidens to not scrutinize.
For what is the lot
The Almighty has got
For all those who do otherwise?

"It's ruin, is it not, for the wicked
And disaster for those who are wretched?
Does not the Almighty
My ways see and tally
Each step, whether straight or else crooked?

"If ever I've rushed with alacrity
To falsehood and cheating and vanity,
Let me be weighed
On scales rightly made,
So that God may know my integrity.

"If my footstep from His path has turned,
If my heart with desire has burned,
If my hands have a spot,
Let my harvest then rot
And another eat what I have earned.

"If my heart's been enticed or seduced
Or my neighbor if I have abused,
Let my wife serve another
And others sleep with her,
For iniquity cannot be excused.

"Let the fire of judgment consume
My increase and all of my boom.
When servants complained
And their cause I disdained
To face God how can I presume?

"When He punishes me, how will I
Give Him a proper reply?
The same way that He
In the womb fashioned me
My servants were also made by.

"If I've caused any widow to moan
Or eaten my food on my own,
Ignoring the orphan—
But I've been a champion
Of the poor since before I was grown.

"If I've seen a man perish uncovered
And haven't his last blessing heard
Or beaten the fatherless,
Let my body be armless,
For disaster from God I have feared.

"If I've made gold my hope and my confidence
Or rejoiced at my wealth and my opulence,
If the sun and the moon
Beguiled me to swoon,
It would be a sin against Providence.

"If I've relished my enemy's downfall
Or gloated when evil did call
On him—but indeed
I never did plead
That curses would hold him in thrall.

"If the men of my tent haven't said,
'Which guest here has not been well-fed?'
But no traveler stayed
In the street, for I made
Available both food and a bed.

"My sins I did not hide like Adam,
Concealing them inside my bosom.
For fear of the loud
Scorns of the crowd
I did not lie low or keep mum.

"Oh, that I had one to hear me!
Here, my name's signed on my plea.
I wish my Prosecutor
Would give me an answer
In a book written by the Almighty!

"On my shoulder I surely would carry it,
As a crown on my head it would fit.
I'd give an account
Of my footsteps' amount
And prince-like before Him submit.

"If my land and its fields weep against me
For I've eaten its fruit without money
And the ownership bleeds,
Let thistles and weeds
Grow instead, not wheat and barley."

PART VI

Job's Fourth Frenemy

Job 32-37

Elihu further answered and said:
"Hear my words, you wise men;
Give ear to me, you who have knowledge.
For the ear tests words
As the palate tastes food.
Let us choose justice for ourselves;
Let us know among ourselves what is good.
For Job has said, 'I am righteous,
But God has taken away my justice;
Should I lie concerning my right?
My wound is incurable, though I am without transgression.'
What man is like Job,
Who drinks scorn like water,
Who goes in company with the workers of iniquity,
And walks with wicked men?"

–Job 34:1-8

Elihu Begs Leave to Speak

JOB 32:1–33:7

At the end of Job's final lament
His three friends were totally silent,
And this was because
He apparently was
Righteous in his own eyes and judgment.

Then the wrath of a certain Elihu,
The son of one Barachel who
Belonged to the fam
Of a Buzite called Ram,
Against Job was roused and did spew.

He felt that Job did justify
Himself and not God the Most High.
He also was angry
At each of the three
Who judged Job without a reply.

Because they were older than he,
He awaited his turn with propriety.
He thought they'd reply
But they didn't comply
So he spoke up, and long-windedly.

"I'm young and you're all very old,
That's why I wasn't so bold.
For how could I dare
My views to declare
And let my opinions unfold?

"Age, I believe, should speak first
For age is with wisdom well-versed.
But we all have a spirit
And God alone makes it
With good understanding to burst.

"Great men aren't always so wise,
And nor do the aged realize
Often what is
True, proper justice,
So hear me as I verbalize.

"I'll also declare my opinion,
As I heeded while you all did reason.
Your words I awaited
As you deliberated
With Job in your long communication.

"I heard all your speeches attentively,
And not even one of you plainly
Persuaded Job here
Or gave him a clear
Reply, and I did listen closely.

"You should not say, 'Wisdom we've found.
Now God and not man will confound.'
Since Job did not argue
With me but with you
Your speeches I will not resound.

"They're quiet for they are dismayed
And that's why their words do evade.
I waited but they
Stood still and did say
No more, for their answers did fade.

"Therefore I'll answer my part
And my own opinion impart.
I'm so full of words,
And propelled I am onwards
By my spirit to lay bare my heart.

"My belly indeed is like wine
That's bottled up and does incline
To burst into speech
And relief thus to reach,
So I must open these lips of mine.

"Now let me not show partiality
To those who are part of humanity.
And for that matter
Let me not flatter,
Or my Maker will take me quite swiftly.

"But please, Job, do hear this my speech
And carefully listen to each
Of my words as I open
My mouth and have spoken
Knowledge that's pure just like bleach.

"The Spirit of God did create me,
My life's breath is from the Almighty.
If you have an answer
Your words set in order
And take your stand stouteartedly.

"I'm spokesman for you Job today,
For I too am formed out of clay.
Fear not, for I
Will not terrify,
And my hand will not heavily weigh.

Elihu Upbraids Job

JOB 33:8–34:9

"I heard you because I was present.
Your own voice did say, 'I am innocent.
I'm also pristine
And sinless and clean.
In me all transgression is absent.

"'Yet He finds occasions against me
And treats me as He would an enemy.
My both feet He locks
In shackles and stocks
And watches my actions intently.'

"Behold, you are wrong and here's why:
God's much greater than you or I.
So why do you fight
And contend with His might?
His ways He will not justify.

"God speaks in one way or another
Yet humans can never decipher.
He may speak at night
When people sleep tight,
While on their cots they do slumber.

"In a dream or in some nighttime vision
God opens their ears to instruction
To turn them aside
From sin and their pride,
To save them from certain destruction.

"Man's chastened with pain on his bed
As pain in his bones does fast spread.
His soul cannot bear
The choicest of fare,
In which state he hates even bread.

"His flesh wastes away from the blight,
His bones sticking out in plain sight.
His soul then draws near
The Pit's last frontier
And his slayers are ready to smite.

"If there's an appointed mediator
To guide this man as would a tutor,
Then since God is gracious
He'll ransom victorious
His life from the Pit's deathly crater.

"His flesh will renew like a baby's.
He'll return to his youth's early glories,
And then when he prays
He shall see God's face
And thus be restored by God's mercies.

"After this he'll behold other men
And say, 'I committed sin when
What's right I disdained
And so nothing gained.'
His eyes on the light shall gaze then.

"You see, God does work all things twice,
And sometimes He does even thrice,
To bring back man's soul
From the Pit's pitch black hole
So his life will by light become nice.

"Give ear, Job, and listen to me,
And speak, if you must speak, directly.
For I desire to
Justify you
And wisdom impart with sagacity.

"Give ear to my words, O you wise,
And hear me as I vocalize.
The ear does test speech
As the palate does each
Morsel of food that it tries.

"Let's choose for ourselves what is right
And together acquire true insight.
Whatever is just
And good we all must
Learn, to discern dark from light.

"For Job has declared, 'I am righteous,
But God has removed from me justice.
My wound will not cure
Though I'm truly pure.
Should I tell lies concerning my charges?'

"Job drinks down scorn like it's water
And with wicked men he does saunter,
For does he not say,
'It does not pay
To take joy in God our Creator'?

Elihu Defends God's Justice

"Therefore to me kindly listen:
Far be it from God that He sin.
Each one He repays
Based on their ways.
By their deeds He rewards all our kin.

"God never will wickedly act.
His justice is always intact.
Who appointed Him over
The world as its ruler?
Who offered to Him such a contract?

"If God should His heart set upon it
And remove from earth's ambit His Spirit,
In an instant all flesh
Together would perish
And dust they would quickly revisit.

"If you have discernment then hear this:
Should one rule who does not love justice?
Will you deem as guilty
The just God Almighty?
A king can you tell, 'You are worthless'?

"You won't scorn the noble official,
But God is completely impartial.
Both rich and poor
He regards alike for
As the work of His hands they are special.

"In the dead of the night they will die,
In barely the blink of an eye.
The people are shaken
When princes are taken
Without a hand or a goodbye.

"God watches the ways of each one.
He sees everything they have done.
There's no kind of darkness
Where workers of vileness
Can hide or from Him far off run.

"God does not need more to consider
A man or examine him further.
He shatters the mighty
Without any inquiry
And instead of them sets up another.

"The doings of all men He knows
And them in the night overthrows,
Striking them dead
If they have been wicked,
Which action to others He shows.

"Because they had all turned away
And did not give heed to His way,
To God's ear the cries
Of the poor ones did rise,
For He hears when afflicted men pray.

"When God does bestow peace and quietness
Who'll dare to bring trouble and menace
Against any nation
Or those in seclusion?
Thus no one's ensnared by the godless.

"Has anyone said, 'I have sinned
But now I have been disciplined.
I'll offend You no more
And if I'm impure
Do show me what I must rescind'?

"On your terms should He recompense
And that way His justice dispense?
It's all your decision
So share your position.
Go on, let me hear your defense.

"Men who are wise have been telling me:
'Job has been speaking unknowingly.
His statements are lacking
Discernment's sound backing.'
Thus they have said to me personally.

"Oh, that this Job would be tried
To the utmost because he replied
Just like wicked men,
And in his rebellion
Has words against God multiplied!

"Do you think it is right that you say,
'My righteousness does far outweigh
The Lord God's' and 'Does
My cleanness help us
More than if I'd gone astray?'

"I'll answer you, Job, and your friends.
Look up as your vision ascends.
The clouds in the sky
Above you are high
And heaven beyond them extends.

"If you do wrong what do you accomplish?
And if your transgressions do flourish
Does God feel distressed?
Or is He impressed
When you're righteous and free from all blemish?

"Your sin affects humans like you
And the same does your righteousness too.
When oppressions increase
Men shout for release.
From the arm of the strong they seek rescue.

"But no one says, 'Where is my Maker,
The God who's my nighttime song-giver?
Which beasts that do roar
Or birds that do soar
Can teach us, for He makes us wiser?'

"They're teeming with wicked men's vanity.
Their talk is but foolish and empty,
So that when they cry
God will not reply.
Ignored they'll be by the Almighty.

"Your case now before Him is set.
His justice you must wait to get.
Because He's not angrily
Punished your folly
You speak on and will not keep quiet.

Elihu Asserts God's Power

JOB 36:1–23

"Indulge me a bit and I'll show
More knowledge of God, and I'll go
A long way to get it.
My Maker I'll credit,
For truly my words are not pseudo.

"One perfect in knowledge is with you.
Behold, God is mighty, it's true.
He's strong and He's wise
And none He'll despise
But justice will give where it's due.

"The righteous He is watching over
To seat them on kings' thrones forever.
If they are enchained,
By affliction restrained,
Their work and their sins He'll uncover.

"He opens their ear to correction
And tells them to turn from transgression.
If they choose to obey
And serve Him then they
Will prosper throughout their duration.

"Their life will be joyful and pleasant,
But those who remain disobedient
Will reap this reward:
They'll die by the sword
And knowledge in them will be absent.

"God's anger has been set apart
For those with a hypocrite's heart.
They'll die in their youth
Among the uncouth,
With perverted ones they will depart.

"God delivers the poor from affliction
And teaches those facing oppression.
He would have indeed
Steered you from need
To a broad place where there's no restriction.

"With choice fare you would have been fed
But judgment fills your life instead.
Because wrath is there
Watch out and beware,
Lest with a blow you're struck dead.

"You won't get away with a ransom,
For riches can't purchase your freedom.
Or will your vast forces
Stave off distresses?
Therefore the darkness don't welcome.

"It's at nighttime when people are taken.
Be careful Job, for you have chosen
This sinful death-wish.
You rather would perish
Than gracefully bear your affliction.

"Behold, God's exalted in might.
Who teaches like Him with delight?
And who can assign
His pathways or whine,
'God, You've done wrong and not right'?

Elihu Praises God's Works

JOB 36:24–37:24

"Remember the Lord's work to praise,
For upon it does everyone gaze.
Behold, He is great
And none can enumerate
His years, for they truly amaze.

"He draws up the water before
The rain from above He'll down pour
Profusely on land.
Who can understand
How clouds spread and thunder does roar?

"He scatters His light on His canopy
And covers the depths of the sea.
He judges the nations
And gives them provisions
Of nourishment always abundantly.

"With lightning He covers His hands
And where it should strike He commands.
His thunder will follow
And cattle will bellow,
Declaring the storm in the grasslands.

"My heart at this trembles and stumbles.
Just hear when His voice loudly rumbles!
He renders it forth
To the ends of the earth
As a roar, not in faint little mumbles.

"Thus God with His voice clearly thunders.
We can't comprehend His great wonders.
To the snow He will say,
'Fall here today.'
Likewise to the rainfall that launders.

"He brings to a standstill each hand,
That all will His work understand.
The beasts in lairs hide
As breezes do glide
From their chambers to blow upon land.

"By the breath of God cold ice is given
And same way the waters are frozen.
His bright clouds He'll scatter
And fill up with moisture
The rain clouds so they're heavy-laden.

"They twirl, being swirled by His guidance,
His bidding to do in obedience.
Each part of this action
Is for our correction,
Or to show us His mercy and providence.

"O Job, now you really must hear me.
Stand still for a moment and silently
God's works please consider.
Do you know whither
He sends His clouds shining so brightly?

"Do you know why they perfectly waft
And it's sweltering when the wind soft
From southwards does blow?
And did you spread also
The skies like a mirror aloft?

"Teach us to pray, because darkness
Is in us and we are quite clueless.
If we ask God directly
To speak, we will promptly
Be swallowed alive, it is doubtless.

"No person can look at the sunlight
When the skies are all clear, blue, and bright.
The north sky does render
God's golden splendor,
But of God Himself we can't catch sight.

"His power and justice are excellent.
He does not oppress in His judgment.
We all fear Him therefore,
And He will ignore
Those who think they're wise and prudent."

PART VII

GOD'S GOODNESS

JOB 38-42

Then the LORD answered Job out of the whirlwind,
and said:
"Now prepare yourself like a man;
I will question you, and you shall answer Me:
Would you indeed annul My judgment?
Would you condemn Me that you may be justified?
Have you an arm like God?
Or can you thunder with a voice like His?
Then adorn yourself with majesty and splendor,
And array yourself with glory and beauty.
Disperse the rage of your wrath;
Look on everyone who is proud, and humble him."

–Job 40:6-11

Were You Around?

JOB 38:1–38

Out of the whirlwind's great blast
The Lord did Job answer at last.
He said, "Who is this
Whose ignorant speeches
On My wisdom have such darkness cast?

"So brace now yourself like a man
And make a reply if you can.
Were you around
When earth I did found
According to a special floor plan?

"Do you know every fine line's degree?
The earth's cornerstone did you see?
You heard when the stars
Sang out their first bars
And heaven's hosts shouted with glee?

"Who shut in the sea behind doors,
Restricting its haughty waves' course?
With darkness and cloud
I did it enshroud
And limited its vast sandy shores.

"Have you ever commanded the morn
Or ordered it since you were born?
The dawn have you told
Of the earth to take hold
So wickedness can be withdrawn?

"Like a seal on a large lump of clay
Earth's form does the daylight display.
Like a robe it stands out
And the people who flout
God's laws are removed from the way.

"The light of the wicked is taken
At once when the morning has broken.
The person whose arm
Is raised to do harm
Is stopped, for the world has awoken.

"Have you entered the springs of the sea
Or fathomed the deep's mystery?
If the gateways of death
And earth's massive breadth
You can comprehend, then do tell Me.

"Can you map out where daylight does dwell?
The place darkness goes, can you tell?
Are you able to order
It back to its border,
For your decades and years grow and swell?

"Have you entered the treasury of snow
Or of hail, and perchance did you know
I've reserved them both for
The season of war,
When trouble will cast its long shadow?

"Do you know what way light is diffused
Or how earth with wind is suffused?
Who has for water
And bolts of loud thunder
Their channels and pathways produced?

"Who caused it to rain on a soil
Where people will nevermore toil,
Its parchedness to slake
So that grass will make
The dry desolation recoil?

"Does rain that descends have a father?
Do dewdrops and ice have a mother?
And who has begotten
The hoar frost of heaven
So water will freeze in cold weather?

"The Pleiades' chains can you bind
Or the belt of Orion unwind?
The Bear can you guide
With cubs at its side?
Do you know how the skies were designed?

"Do the clouds sprinkle at your command?
Does lightning go where you demand?
And who did impart
To a mere mortal's heart
The wisdom to think or understand?

"Who can count the innumerable crowds
Of thick, water-laden storm clouds?
When clumps of dust harden
Then who from high heaven
The earth with its rainfall enshrouds?"

Do You Know?

JOB 38:39–39:30

Now after the physical world
The Lord in Job's hearing unfurled
His manifold wisdom
Of the animal kingdom
So his mind in amazed wonder swirled.

"Can you hunt for the young lions' prey
In thickets and dens as they lay,
Lurking in wait
Their hunger to sate?
And who feeds the ravens each day?

"When she-goats give birth do you know?
Or when it is time for the doe
To bring forth her child
Out there in the wild?
Do you know how this happens also?

"These mothers bow down to the earth
And that's how they give their young birth.
The offspring grow strong
And before very long
They depart from home's sheltering girth.

"Who gave the wild donkey his liberty?
He despises the noise of the city
And refuses to follow
The driver's loud bellow,
For the wasteland his lodging must be.

"His home I've created the wilderness
And the barren land's his natural recess.
The mountainous range
Is the onager's grange,
Where he searches for every green cress.

"Will the feral ox willingly serve you
And slumber in your manger too?
Can you tie him with ropes
To plow land in hopes
He'll return with your grain when he's through?

"Will you trust him because he is great
In might and can shoulder the weight
Of your labor adeptly,
And then from the valley
To the threshing floor carry your freight?

"The wings of the ostrich flap proudly
But she handles her young very harshly,
Leaving her eggs
Where anyone's legs
Can crush and destroy them quite easily.

"The Lord has deprived her of sense
For He did not endow her with prudence.
And yet when this bird
Lifts herself upward
She outpaces the horse any distance.

"That galloper did you endue
With power, or can you subdue
The horse like an insect?
Fear has no effect
On him, he can armies pursue.

"He doesn't turn back from the battle.
The quiver against him does rattle.
The glittering spear
And javelin are near
As he charges to clashing of metal.

"The distance he eats up with rage
And will not stop or disengage
At the trumpeter's blare.
From afar he's aware
Of the war that the captains do wage.

"Does your wisdom the hawk cause to fly?
Does the eagle its home make on high
At your behest?
From its lofty nest
This raptor its prey does espy.

"On the crag of the rock it resides.
On strongholds it swoops and it glides.
When people are slain
The eaglets will drain
Blood from the corpses' insides."

.

Can You Also?

JOB 40:1–14

Having given this detailed description
Of His intimate grasp of creation,
The Lord did moreover
Provide Job an answer
In the form of a plainspoken question.

"Shall the person who wants to contend
With the Lord God Almighty intend
To give Him correction
For some imperfection?
Let that person himself now defend."

Whereupon Job said, "Lord, I am vile.
I spoke once or twice but now I'll
Position my hand
Upon my lips and
My tongue will stay still and immobile."

As Job sat in his humbled silence
Out of the same tempest's turbulence
The Lord spoke once more
As He'd done before,
With questions convicting Job's conscience.

"My justice would you nullify,
Condemn Me to self-justify?
Is your arm as stout?
Can you also shout
Like thunder that peals in the sky?

"If so, then yourself deck with majesty.
Be arrayed with rich splendor and beauty.
Go on a rampage
In unbridled rage
So the proud get a taste of humility.

"Trample the base where they stand
And bury them all in the sand.
Dispatch them to darkness
And then I'll confess
That you can be saved by your hand."

Behemoth and Leviathan

JOB 40:15–41:34

And then the Lord went on to share
A few things He knew of a pair
Of creatures so large
That no man could charge
At them, even if he did dare.

The first was Behemoth, a beast
Who on grass like the oxen did feast.
The next was Leviathan,
Whose fierce disposition
Could never be tamed in the least.

"See now, this Behemoth's strength lies
In his hips and his muscular thighs.
His tail's like a cedar
And his body's bones are
Like iron or bronze beams in size.

"The foremost of God's works created,
His Maker alone has mandated
That he may come near
His sword without fear.
By others he won't be dictated.

"Where the beasts of the fields play he feeds.
The mountains give him what he needs.
In the lotus tree glade
He's covered with shade
As he lounges by willows and reeds.

"The Jordan flows by him in spate
Yet Behemoth does not agitate.
The river is rapid
But he remains placid,
Beholding it in a calm state.

"Could you draw Leviathan out
With a hook, or a stalk through his snout
Pierce, or adorn
His jaw with a thorn,
His tongue to ensnare from without?

"Will this creature beseech you for mercy
Or speak to you ever so softly,
Or make an agreement
To work as your servant
And wait on you all through eternity?

"Will you play with him as with a bird
Or show him to maidens untethered?
Will your trade partners try
Like merchants to buy
Leviathan so he can be severed?

"With harpoons his skin can you fill?
His head with your spears can you drill?
Do not touch him for
You will lose the war!
The odds of you winning are nil.

"If the sight of him chills every spine
What person could ever incline
The Lord God to counter?
I'm no person's debtor.
Each thing under heaven is Mine.

"Leviathan does have a fine frame
And his outer coat's also the same.
His firm scales he wields
Like a proud row of shields,
Close-set and not easy to maim.

"Who can open the doors of his face
Where his terrible teeth have a place?
Between every scale
In his taut coat of mail
Even air cannot find a small space.

"Like the lids of the morning's first light
His eyes gleam and glister so bright.
From out of his maw
And tightly clenched jaw
His sneezings like fire ignite.

"They flash forth and spray from his nostrils
Like a smoke cloud that billows and spirals
Out from a pot
That's boiling and hot,
And charcoals his blazing breath kindles.

"Strength in his thick neck does dwell
And before him despondence does swell.
His flesh is quite firm.
Its folds do not squirm,
Being snugly encased in their shell.

"His heart is as flinty as stone.
Compassion to him is unknown.
When he does arise
Big vessels capsize
And the mighty in terror do moan.

"The sword over him can't prevail.
The javelin and dart also fail,
For bronze is as wood
And iron only could
Him injure as straw in a bale.

"The arrow can't force him to flee
And slingstones as chaff he does see.
No fierce pointed dart
Can pierce near his heart
And at lances he glances with glee.

"His belly, like pieces of pottery,
Leaves marks in the place that is miry.
He makes the deep roil
Like a pot on the boil,
A cauldron of ointment that's watery.

"The sea by his sharp jagged underside
Does shine with a hoary-haired tide.
On earth there is nothing
Like him who is king
Over all of the children of pride."

With these words the Lord finished speaking.
Although He had not said a thing
On the problem of pain,
Job did ascertain
God's glory transcended his suffering.

Job's Restoration

JOB 42

Then Job thus did answer the Lord:
"You can do everything and no word
Or purpose of Yours,
Not even by force,
Can anyone hinder or thwart.

"I said what I didn't understand,
Things that were for me very grand.
Yet I ask You humbly
Please listen to me,
For Your words do an answer demand.

"I've heard by the ear that You're wise
But now I can see with my eyes.
Therefore I must
In ashes and dust
Repent, for myself I despise."

The Lord later said to the Temanite,
"I'm angry with you and the Shuhite.
The Naamathite too,
For all three of you
Did not speak of Me what was right.

"Now go to My servant Job bearing
Bulls and rams as a burnt offering.
His prayer I'll accept,
Or else your inept
Actions will discipline bring."

The men did what God had decreed
And Job did for them intercede.
God then blessed him double
For all of his trouble,
And the guests who arrived he did feed.

There were brothers and sisters of his,
And those who had been old acquaintances.
As Job they consoled
They gave rings of gold,
And he also received silver pieces.

The Lord in this manner did bless
Job latterly more and not less,
With sheep and with oxen
And camels, and seven
Sons all of this to possess.

And the three daughters he fathered
Most beauteous in Uz were considered.
The first was Jemimah,
The next was Keziah,
And Keren-Happuch was the third.

Once these things had all taken place
Job fourteen whole decades did grace
The earth, and saw even
His children's grandchildren,
Then died old and chockfull of days.

EPILOGUE

The Purpose of Pain

We also glory in tribulations, knowing that tribulation produces perseverance; and perseverance, character; and character, hope. Now hope does not disappoint, because the love of God has been poured out in our hearts by the Holy Spirit who was given to us.

—Romans 5:3-5

My brethren, count it all joy when you fall into various trials, knowing that the testing of your faith produces patience. But let patience have its perfect work, that you may be perfect and complete, lacking nothing.

—James 1:2-4

Therefore let those who suffer according to the will of God commit their souls to Him in doing good, as to a faithful Creator.

—1 Peter 4:19

Primary Purposes of Pain

And now in this book's final bit
Let me aim like an archer to hit
The target, bull's-eye,
So I may justify
Why affliction does pay us a visit.

Our suffering has purpose, you know,
Though often it doesn't seem so.
Regardless, when we
See life biblically
We'll learn something from every sorrow.

What follows is not all-inclusive,
But I hope that it will be persuasive.
I've selected the three
I believe are the primary
Purposes of pain that are positive.

Purpose 1: Pain Pushes Us to God

Often till life becomes bleak
God's presence we don't care to seek.
It will take a trial
To get us to dial
His emergency line, so to speak.

In times when we think we don't need God
Our manner with Him can be slipshod.
Like wandering sheep
His paths we don't keep
Until tapped by the Good Shepherd's rod.

God does not in our pain take pleasure.
The problems we face aren't a measure
That He is irate
But there's no debate
That communion with us He does treasure.

When down if we'll offer up praise
We'll find that our Father is always
Present with us.
No trouble or fuss
Can hinder us from His embrace.

God's nearness is what we require
When forces against us conspire.
In grief when we groan
We can't be alone,
For alone one might sink in quagmire.

When we anxiously open the Bible
We'll discover it's perfectly able
Our mind to renew
And alter us too
By showing us how not to stumble.

Our spirit does not live by bread
But rather our spirit is fed
By every word
The mouth of the Lord
Has said, so the Word must be read.

Each one needs to better relate
With the Father who did us create
For close fellowship.
In moments of worship
We'll see that He's both good and great.

Some imagine God's one or the other.
Perhaps He's too splendid to bother
With mere mortal men.
It's no wonder then
They think He's a mean cosmic monster.

And some people have a propensity
For picturing God as a deity
Who obeys our commands
And meets our demands
Like a doting grandmother or aunty.

These opinions are equally askew.
The Lord we must all learn to view
As both great and good
And each trial should
Our mind and perspective renew.

Yes, God is loving and tender
Yet He is able to render
The discipline needed
If Him we've not heeded,
Much more as a frequent offender.

A teacher or college professor
Will examine us in an endeavor
To discover if we
Truly did study
And whether the lesson did master.

Wouldn't God do the same thing also?
Like teachers won't He need to know
If we've understood
What He for our good
Has taught us, which testing will show?

Naturally not every test
Is God on a curricular quest.
But if the exam
Is on His program
Then to ace it we will do our best.

Purpose 2: Pain Purifies Our Faith

In good times so often are we
Believers pretending to be.
But when in a trial,
Like through a glass vial
The state of our faith all can see.

On occasion our faith is too frail.
It buckles when we're in travail.
Faith cannot be strong
If its object is wrong
And we put it in gods that will fail.

We don't need so large of a quantity
But simply the right kind of quality.
A faith that's mature
Will help us endure,
For it has passed God's standard of purity.

Gold that is placed in the fire
May feel the refiner's full ire,
But it's only the dross
He wishes to toss
Because it's admixture and mire.

The ore must be fully refined
So impurities will be consigned
To the blistering flames
As the furnace reclaims
The dross, and the gold's left behind.

The refiner intends for the gold
Before being poured in a mold
To come out so pure
That he will be sure
In it his own face to behold.

Our faith is more precious, that's why
When hurting it's helpful to try
To bear this in mind
God isn't unkind,
And to let Him our faith purify.

By faith did the patriarchs of old
Invisible promises behold.
By faith even they
Did trust and obey,
And that's why their stories are told.

By faith righteous Abel did bring
The fat of his flock as an offering.
By faith did Enoch
With God daily walk
And was taken instead of expiring.

By faith Noah always lived upright
And that gave God ample delight.
He built a big boat,
An ark that could float,
Before rain was known or in sight.

By faith also Abraham the great
Did with the Almighty relate
As one with a friend
From beginning to end,
An example we must imitate.

By faith barren Sarah, his wife,
Though well past her childbearing life
At ninety received
Strength and conceived
The son who was saved from the knife.

For God would tell Abraham to lay
Isaac on the altar and slay
His dearly loved son,
And this thing was done
To determine if he would obey.

By faith Abraham did pass the test,
And before his knife could touch the chest
Isaac was spared,
For God had prepared
A ram, as the Scriptures attest.

There are many examples like these
In the Bible, and they are the keys
That help us unlock
The blessings in stock,
Things faith and obedience release.

Purpose 3: Pain Prunes Our Character

Pain always will birth things of beauty
When permitted to finish its duty.
We know works of art
Sometimes have a start
In a season of tears and adversity.

Or think how a natural pearl
Is formed when the irritants swirl
Inside of an oyster
And continue to fester
Till a gem from the shell can unfurl.

The best work of art is our character
And suffering is often the factor
That takes out the ugly
And makes us more lovely,
Far kinder to all we encounter.

The Lord, like a good gold refiner,
Is making our character finer
So as in pure gold
The world will behold
In us just the Master Designer.

Refining, this fact's undeniable,
Is how we become truly pliable.
And during the process
We learn to fret less,
To be patient, composed, and reliable.

Through trials we acquire perseverance,
Which allows us to go the full distance.
This earthly race isn't
A dash or a sprint
But a marathon requiring endurance.

Our trials must get us to drop
Bad habits we know we should stop.
The big and the small
Let's shed each and all,
Like leaves falling from a treetop.

The rosebush that blossoms in June
The gardener months earlier must prune.
Only then will its roses
Enrapture our noses
And its beauty the garden festoon.

The vine that produces fine grapes
By pruning the vinedresser shapes.
It is the same picture
In all horticulture.
No fruit tree this pruning escapes.

Pruning is part of preparation
For our destiny and our promotion.
The one who's mature
God will trust with more
And call to a higher position.

In us God is seeking maturity
Because when we enter eternity
With Him we will reign,
And thus all our pain
Is fitting us for royalty.

A boy who by birth is a prince
Is raised in a special way since
He will rule someday
Over those who obey,
So his training does not make him wince.

We are being groomed for a kingdom
That's eternal, so we should with wisdom
For it prepare,
Taking great care
That our manner's not reckless or random.

We always must take the long view
When troubles we chance to go through.
This tableau is merely
A rehearsal and we
Are actors awaiting our cue.

Our problems will not last forever,
For life is a brief fleeting vapor.
By fixing our eyes
On the heavenly prize
With joy we'll endure what we suffer.

Conclusion

Therefore when all's said and done
No person concludes pain is fun,
But often indeed
It is what we need
To become more like God's only Son.

If we're real disciples of His
Our predestination is this:
His image to bear,
His attitude to share,
And humbly perform our Lord's service.

Although He in nature was deity
He did not consider equality
With God a position
To grasp, as His mission
Was to lay down His life for humanity.

To strike on the head of the serpent
He appeared in the form of a servant.
Being found as a man
He followed God's plan
Even though crucifixion it meant.

He was scorned and rejected by men,
Acquainted with grief and forsaken,
A Man of sorrows
Who for our woes
Was afflicted and wounded and stricken.

Our iniquity did punishment yield,
But as ancient prophecy revealed
He was penalized,
For our peace chastised,
And by His stripes we have been healed.

We all are like sheep that have strayed
From the paths that for us had been made.
We've turned, everyone,
Our own will we've done,
And on Him our transgressions were laid.

He was led as a lamb to the slaughter.
As the ewe is in front of her shearer
So He too was silent,
This Suffering Servant.
Not a word from His mouth did He utter.

His body was bruised and nail-scarred,
Beyond recognition was marred
By human hand,
And then from the land
Of the living was roughly debarred.

With the wicked dispatched to the grave,
He was laid in the rich man's enclave.
Because He did die
For lawbreakers by
His knowledge He many shall save.

He poured out His soul as an offering
For sin unto death, nothing sparing.
What God has decreed
Through Him shall succeed,
And surely He shall see His offspring.

One day His name shall be heard
In praises forever unhindered.
All earth will acclaim
And heaven will proclaim:
"Worthy is the Man who suffered!"

TETELESTAI

Afterword

Prior to this writing, I had read Job in its entirety only twice—and the second instance was back in 1997. I'd go over my favorite bits occasionally, but to my shame there was no complete reading in the quarter-century before I began this book. The pendulum then swung the other way. I read every chapter several times while composing Parts I–VII, consulting parallel versions, commentaries, and Strong's Interlinear Bible. For the sake of convenience I will refer to these multiple instances collectively as the third reading.

Initial Impressions

Being in my teens when I first read Job, much of what transpires between chapters 2 and 42 was lost on me. I thought Job's friends were right and Job was wrong, and I was aghast that the character who famously says "The Lord gave, and the Lord has taken away" in the opening chapter would, on the very next page, be cursing the day of his birth.

I had myself been nursing a secret death-wish since the age of twelve, when my father said something that crushed me. It took years for me to admit this and be set free, but when I read Job as a teenager I was shocked that its protagonist actually expresses his death-wish aloud. And I was offended that the Bible contained the words I thought God didn't know I thought: "*Why did I not die at birth?*" (3:11).

God Himself was not exempt from my adolescent interrogations. Notwithstanding what we are told in the opening narrative, why did God let Job suffer in this fashion? And why didn't He at least inform him about Satan's bid for his soul? Surely it would have helped the poor man endure his terrible affliction? And when God finally speaks in the whirlwind, why doesn't He offer Job any tender expressions of comfort? And why a *whirlwind* of all things? Couldn't the One who created the heavens and the earth have spoken to Job in the kind of gentle breeze I imagined wafting across the green pastures in Psalm 23?

I did not read Job again until my late twenties, six years into my journey of inner healing. I was living with my parents in Mumbai and the Sri Lankan writer Vinoth Ramachandra, whom I had met at a literary picnic on Gorai Beach, had sent me a copy of his new book, *Gods That Fail*. When I finished the chapter titled "Job & The Silence of God," I turned to the Book of Job again.[1]

My second reading was less naïve. For one thing, I no longer agreed with Job's friends, having discerned that much of what they say, though not necessarily wrong, was not *right*, for it came from a limited and even secondhand knowledge of God. I now understood why the Lord had told Eliphaz, "You have not spoken of Me what is right" (42:7). But I remained baffled by the next clause: "as My servant Job has."

Job had spoken *rightly* about God? Had I misread chapters 3 to 31 *again*?

Truth be told, I still found the bulk of Job's speeches unworthy of a man held up as a paragon of patience and perseverance, as we know from James 5:10–11. Yet, as I look back on that second reading, I can see that I was inching towards the heart of Job: the apparent absence of God in the presence of pain. This central concern of Job is a key problem of pain.[2]

In the introduction I had said that the question sufferers most often ask is, *Why am I suffering?* But that is merely the overt query. Whether we realize it or not, the true cry of our heart is, *Where is God as I am suffering?* For even if we knew every last reason for our predicament, it would not comfort us as much as knowing that God is with us.[3]

Job is no different. At one point he despairingly sighs, "Oh, that I knew where I might find Him, That I may come to His seat!" (23:3). He mistakenly thinks that when he "finds" God he will argue his case and get the justice he deserves, for nothing of the sort ends up happening. But my point is, Job knows he needs the presence of God. The presence of these friends of his was fine as long as they were sitting quietly beside him. Once they begin talking, they prove to be "worthless physicians" (13:4) and their company ceases to be comforting. Thus Job is back to seeking the One who has the answers—if He can but be found.[4]

In my second reading I still did not understand why God never addresses the problem of pain when He finally answers Job. But I had been through enough emotional healing by now to grasp the critical truth that *God had given Job the answer Job needed, and that's what mattered.*

Today I am more convinced than ever that when we are suffering we don't need a general, proverbial word, which is the very thing Job accuses his friends of offering him in his misery: as he disgustedly says, "Your platitudes are proverbs of ashes" (13:12).

What we need is a specific and personal word from God—a word that in fact can only be given *by* God.[5]

When God speaks to Job in the whirlwind, revealing a fraction of His infinite knowledge of the natural world, it is spoken to a particular man at a particular point. We have much to glean from God's words to Job, but we cannot expect them to comfort us in our trials. We must ask Him to speak to us in our individual situations, and to trust that He will. For if the Book of Job teaches us anything, it is that at the right time God *will* speak. His silence is but a precursor.

Cold Comforters

In my third reading I was disturbed by the callousness of those closest to Job. At the same time, I was moved that his friends, on hearing of his adversity, made an appointment "to come and mourn with him, and to comfort him" (2:11). This detail had escaped me earlier, but I was now reminded of how three of my own friends had taken turns to be on the phone with me when my mother died. A source of inexpressible consolation on the saddest day of my life, these calls allowed me to appreciate the concern Job's friends display when they set out to commiserate with him.

Eliphaz, Bildad, and Zophar succeed in the first part of their mission, to mourn with Job. When they see from afar how affliction has disfigured him, they weep aloud, and each tears his robe and sprinkles dust on his head toward heaven as a sign of sorrow. Then they sit on the ground beside him for a whole week, not saying a word to him, "for they saw that his grief was very great" (2:13). If anything conveys the enormity of Job's suffering, it is this seven-day silence of solidarity. His suffering has not only made grown men weep, it has rendered them speechless.

Where the friends fail is in the mission to *comfort* Job. Once they break their silence, what follows is a barrage of harsh, unmerited accusations, driving Job to denounce them as "miserable comforters" (16:2). In English at least, the epithet "Job's comforter" has come to mean "a person who discourages or depresses while seemingly giving comfort and consolation."[6]

My teenage assessment of Job's friends was partly correct. At face value, their proverbial statements about the wicked are not wrong. But during this writing I realized that *they are actually accusing Job of being that wicked man!* With friends like these who needs enemies?[7]

As I plowed through their stream of rehearsed clichés and insipid platitudes, I got the impression that Eliphaz, Bildad, and Zophar want Job to simply acknowledge his guilt and shut up. In typical male fashion, they seem uneasy with their friend's emotional outburst. But any sense of female superiority I may have felt evaporated the minute I saw that the most despicable thing said to Job in this book *is said by a woman*.

When God gives Satan permission to afflict Job's body and he is struck all over with painful boils, he sits down among the ashes and scrapes himself with a piece of pottery. At this lowest point of his life, his wife makes her sole appearance in the book.

"Do you still hold fast to your integrity?" she asks (2:9), and it's the word *still* that best captures her contempt. She is ironically echoing what God Himself had said when He told Satan, "Still he holds fast to his integrity, though you incited Me against him, to destroy him without cause" (2:3). But whereas "still" was the ultimate compliment when God said it, it is the ultimate insult in Mrs. Job's lips. Instead of commending her husband's uprightness, she derides it. She has lost the same children, servants, property, and status, but trouble has so blinded her that she cannot recognize integrity when it is squarely in front of her. Perched on a garbage dump oozing pus, yes, but integrity nonetheless.[8]

After flinging her contemptuous query, Job's wife tells him to curse God and die. Her belief that he'll be better off renouncing God and going to hell is horrifying enough. What's worse, she is actually defying Job to do the very thing Satan said he would do! Only a few verses earlier Satan had told God, "Stretch out Your hand now, and touch his bone and flesh, *and he will surely curse You to Your face!*" (2:5, italics added).[9]

Job duly rebukes his wife, but we are not told if she repents. He later laments, "My breath is offensive to my wife" (19:17), and refers to her while defending his integrity for the last time (31:10), but she is not mentioned in the book's happy ending. Whether she died and was replaced by someone more worthy, or whether she eventually repented, the Bible is silent.

Enigmatic Elihu

In my previous readings I had somehow overlooked the mysterious character of Elihu, whose existence we become aware of only after Job's closing defense is followed by the brief statement, "The words of Job are ended" (31:40). This time I found the young Buzite particularly tiresome. Early in his speech, when he declares, "I am full of words" (32:18), I knew I was in for a long ride. Yet, even though certain scholars consider Elihu's six chapters an interpolation, I could not omit them because they fit the book so perfectly in dramatic, thematic, and literary terms.[10]

By the time we learn that a fifth man is present, we've had to sit through almost *thirty* chapters of unremitting dialogue. The short narrative that opens Job 32 serves as a welcome relief, though it is disheartening to read about Elihu's wrath four times in this passage. He is rightly angry with the friends, "because they had found no answer, and yet had condemned Job" (32:3), but his anger towards Job seems merciless. Although we are told by way of explanation that this is because Job "justified himself rather than God" (32:2), one cannot but detect a note of self-righteousness in Elihu. And then there's that belabored preamble in which he begs leave to speak and announces that he is going to speak.

Nevertheless, Elihu's speech works brilliantly from the standpoint of technique, for it is connected to the preceding and succeeding speeches through the literary device of repetition. When he repeats what Job and his friends have said, it refreshes the reader's memory. This would have been especially helpful for the early audience, who *listened* to Scripture and could not turn pages back like readers. And towards the end of his speech, when Elihu says things God Himself will say in chapters 38 to 41, it has an anticipatory effect.

Another reason why I could not exclude Elihu's section from my book is because I suspect he is the unnamed author of Job. Perhaps most glaringly, he is the only character whose genealogy is listed—even though he is the only one to whom no one speaks and who is therefore least consequential to the action.

If he is indeed the author, Elihu may have been establishing his credentials by stating that he was "the son of Barachel the Buzite, of the family of Ram" (32:2). A young man of his pedigree, scion of a well-respected clan, would be in the position to both rebuke his elders and write the book. I imagine him sitting in on the debates and being inspired to record them when Job cried out, "Oh, that my words were written! Oh, that they were inscribed in a book!" (19:23).

In the tedious middle section of his speech, Elihu regurgitates many of the platitudes we had heard from Eliphaz, Bildad, and

Zophar, and he levels similar accusations at Job, saying he "drinks scorn like water" (34:7) and "walks with wicked men" (34:8) and "adds rebellion to his sin" (34:37). Given that he never gets a reply, it is possible that Elihu did not actually speak to Job but simply inserted *what he would have said* while compiling the book.

This is only conjecture, of course. But if correct, then despite his insufferable pomposity, we owe Elihu a debt of gratitude for leaving us one of the grandest books in the Bible.

Just Job

During this writing, I finally recognized Job as the hero he is. Having previously thought he was completely wrong, and then not completely *right*, I now saw him as the tragic figures of literature, for he too is a noble, eloquent, and wise protagonist who suffers a terrible reversal.

Described at the outset as "the greatest of all the people of the East" (1:3), Job falls from the pinnacle of prosperity into the abyss of adversity, a contrast that comes through strongly in chapters 29 and 30. "Oh, that I were as in months past, As in the days when God watched over me," he laments (29:2). After recalling those halcyon days of yore, he proceeds to recount what life is like in the dismal present, when he must endure the scorn of younger and more inferior men, "Whose fathers I disdained to put with the dogs of my flock" (30:1). The description that ensues will heighten the effect of his magnificent closing defense in chapter 31.

Job's speeches reveal an astonishing depth of insight into human nature. The segment that opens with him addressing his friends as "forgers of lies" (13:4) proves he has figured out they secretly "show partiality" (13:10) while pretending to be neutral. He has the acuity to see through their "defenses of clay" (13:12).

And his homily in chapter 21 on the prosperity and final destruction of the wicked is among several passages that reflect his moral wisdom, what the Bible often refers to as "understanding."[11]

Job's general knowledge is likewise impressive. He alludes to the natural world on a number of occasions, for example, and he is well acquainted with the plight of the poor (24:5–12) despite being on a higher social level. And the Poem on Wisdom in chapter 28, which opens with a fascinating account of mining, displays Job's extensive grasp of the industry of his day. What makes that speech especially remarkable is how adroitly Job shifts from technology to theology by asking, "But where can wisdom be found? And where is the place of understanding?" (28:12). His questions are answered—by God Himself—in the last verse of that chapter: "Behold, the fear of the Lord, that is wisdom, And to depart from evil is understanding" (28:28).[12]

Job's eloquence is riveting. Unlike the musty clichés of his friends, his language has freshness, vitality, and resonance. And although his speeches are drenched with raw emotion, they are not the garbled ravings of a madman. They are articulate and coherent, sprinkled with vivid, poignant imagery. For instance, he speaks of his brothers vanishing "deceitfully as a brook" (6:15); that his days flee by "like an eagle swooping on its prey" (9:26); and that affliction chokes "as the collar of [his] coat" (30:18). Of the numerous passages that thrilled me from a literary perspective, the most evocative was this:

> For there is hope for a tree,
> If it is cut down, that it will sprout again,
> And that its tender shoots will not cease.
> Though its root may grow old in the earth,
> And its stump may die in the ground,
> Yet at the scent of water it will bud

> And bring forth branches like a plant.
> But man dies and is laid away;
> Indeed he breathes his last
> And where is he? (14:7–10)

I was remembering my mother as I composed the stanzas based on these lines. Later I was amazed to recall an uncannily similar bit in my first book, *Pioneer Boulevard*, which was published in 2013.

> The afternoon sunshine was filtering to the ground in gimlet droplets through the chartreuse leaves and pods of a pepper tree. The tree Vinita loved was returning to life, but she'd never see that miracle again. Hypnotized by the dappled driveway, where light and shadow constantly traded places, the permanence of Vinita's death struck Piyali in a way that neither the corpse nor the empty house had been able to do, despite the tears they'd generated. *Here was this tree, reemerging from death as it would again next year, brimming with so much life that surplus pods dropped to the ground and the green of its leaves quite hurt the eye, whereas her friend—who had laughed and loved and lived as a tree never could—would remain a fine grey powder contained within a couple of cinerary urns.*[13]

Having last read Job in 1997, it was not on my radar in 2013. Yet, perhaps as an intimation of *this* book, I was inspired to add that paragraph before the manuscript went to press. And perhaps as an intimation of the biblical text that bears his name, Job wishes his words were "inscribed in a book" and "engraved on a rock" (19:23–24). Next we have his most famous assertion:

> For I know my Redeemer lives,
> And He shall stand at last on the earth;
> And after my skin is destroyed, this I know,
> That in my flesh I shall see God,

> Whom I shall see for myself,
> And my eyes shall behold, and not another.
> How my heart yearns within me! (19:25–27)

Whether prior to his trial or during it, Job has received the revelation of a living, personal Redeemer whom he will one day see with his own eyes. And thus, much as he'd like to be delivered from his suffering, what his heart yearns for is that he'll be raised from the dead to stand in his Redeemer's presence.[14]

In less hopeful moments, Job is sure he will perish his affliction, but he lives to see another *140 years!* His losses are gloriously restored, and God also gives him a posthumous commendation. In his sole Old Testament mention outside the Book of Job, he is named among those who would have delivered themselves "by their righteousness" (Ezek. 14:14, 14:20). This is not referring to spiritual deliverance or salvation. What God means is that He can find *only three* truly upright Israelites, of whom Job is one.

This should not come as a surprise, for we were told in the opening verse itself that he was "blameless and upright, and one who feared God and shunned evil." Job 1:1 is quoting verbatim what the Lord had said when praising Job before Satan twice, each time adding the tremendous compliment, "*There is none like him on the earth*" (1:8, 2:3). The word translated upright in these verses, *yashar*, is one of my favorite Hebrew words because it is the root of my name Sharon.

As for Job's name, opinion is divided as to its meaning. Some believe it derives from the Hebrew word meaning "the persecuted one," while others think its root is an Arabic term meaning "the repentant one." Whichever is correct, Job lived up to both. He was afflicted to the point that his name has become synonymous with suffering; and despite his countless questions and anguished laments, his final response is one of genuine repentance. After God has finished speaking, Job utters this moving confession:

> I have heard of You by the hearing of the ear,
> But now my eye sees You.
> Therefore I abhor myself,
> And repent in dust and ashes. (42:5–6)

The Hebrew word translated repent, *nacham*, can also mean to console.[15] It appears seven times in the book, but this is the only place where it means to repent. This is fitting, since Job is acknowledging the error of his ways before the Lord.[16]

I have long been fascinated with the messianic foreshadows in the Old Testament, a subject I explored in *The Blessing of Melchizedek*. Like Melchizedek, who is a type of Christ in his kingship and priesthood, Job prefigures Christ in his *sufferings*, for he too is an upright man who suffers innocently and excruciatingly. Interestingly, God four times refers to Job as "My servant" (1:8, 2:3, 42:7–8), the same term He will use for the Messiah in places like Isaiah 52:13 and Zechariah 3:8.

My book's conclusion is based on two of the best-known passages about Christ's sufferings: the messianic prophecy in Isaiah 53 and Paul's hymn in Philippians 2. Writing centuries apart but under divine inspiration, the prophet and the apostle both portray Christ as the servant who willingly suffers in obedience to God. And each ends with a similar declaration: *One day the Man Who Suffered will receive the full reward of His suffering.*

Good God

The highlight of my third reading is that I at last understood God's response to Job. Even the whirlwind made sense this time. Whereas the still small voice was what the prophet Elijah needed as he hid in the cave centuries later, nothing less than a turbulent tempest would adequately console Job on the ash-heap of affliction. As Ramachandra observes:

> The storm both conveys and conceals the fearsome majesty of God. And for the first time since the prologue to the book the author uses the covenant name of Yahweh instead of speaking of God. God is no longer distant and detached, but the gracious and faithful Lord of the covenant. He has been present all along, but now that presence is made known to Job.[17]

The One who created the heavens and the earth with a word speaks like no other, and nowhere do we see this quite like Job 38–41. Interspersed throughout God's many questions we find images that stun by their elegance and precision. Early in His first speech, when God says the earth at dawn "takes on form like clay under a seal" (38:14), it evokes the picture of hills and dales waking to the light of a new day. And in the long last passage God will describe Leviathan's eyes like "the eyelids of the morning" (41:18). The analogy is a surprising one considering how vastly dawn's delicate beauty differs from the sea-monster's warlike ferocity. Yet the mental image once seen cannot be unseen.

The Book of Job reveals the primary aspects of God's character: His goodness and His greatness. Job already knows a thing or two of both. He was blessed abundantly prior to his suffering, and he was aware it had come from God. While rebuking his wife he says, "Shall we indeed accept good from God, and shall we not accept adversity?" (2:10). And he talks knowledgeably of God's power (e.g., 9:5–10, 12:13–24, 26:7–14). But once God begins to speak in the whirlwind, everything Job has known of Him is left in the dust. Could it be that by mentioning Job to Satan and allowing Satan to take the bait, God had this ace up His sleeve all along?

Could it be that this was the end *intended* by the Lord, as James 5:11 says, and not a mere afterthought?

God's speeches leave Job (and us) in no doubt that His sovereignty extends over the entire cosmos, from the farthest reaches of the firmament to every natural phenomenon and living creature. And His knowledge of the world is not just infinite, it's *intimate*. This is especially evident in the passage where God asks Job if he knows when the mountain goats and the deer give birth, then proceeds to describe the process:

> They bow down,
> They bring forth their young,
> They deliver their offspring.
> Their young ones are healthy,
> They grow strong with grain;
> They depart and do not return to them. (39:3–4)

The God who is enthroned in the heavens knows when a lowly mountain goat goes into labor in some remote wilderness on earth! And He watches the kids as they grow, until they are strong enough to strike out on their own. Any parent who has had to send a child out into the world—or out *of* the world, as Job did—will be able to appreciate what is being communicated in this quiet, tender detail.

The opening verses of Job 39 anticipate Jesus's words in the Sermon on the Mount: "Look at the birds of the air, for they neither sow nor reap nor gather into barns; yet your heavenly Father feeds them. Are you not of more value than they?" (Matt. 6:26). It's a rhetorical question, not unlike the many God asks Job.

"What shall I answer You?" replies Job. "I lay my hand over my mouth" (40:4). It was appropriate in the context, but we must respond to Jesus's question with an unequivocal *yes*. As those God so loved that He "did not spare His own Son, but delivered Him up for us all" (Rom. 8:32), *yes*, we are infinitely more valuable than our winged friends, who also enjoy the heavenly Father's care.[18]

Closing Comments

In his insightful volume on suffering, which had profoundly impacted me during the first major crisis of my adulthood, Theodore Epp writes: "In the Book of Job we find one of the greatest records of how God showed His grace to a man who had waited—possibly for years—in a condition of severe suffering."[19]

Whether Job suffered "for years" or not, it probably felt like eons to him, for time tends to drag when we are waiting or suffering. Whatever the actual duration, no one can deny the lavishness of the Lord's grace to Job. And it was a grace twice given: while he was suffering, enabling him to persevere; and afterwards, in the form of a splendid reward.

God's magnanimity is on full display in the book's final chapter. Not only does He graciously accept Job's repentance and his intercession for Eliphaz and company, but He restores him materially too. We told that the Lord "gave Job twice as much as he had before" (42:10), and "blessed the latter days of Job more than his beginning" (42:12).

Job also receives back his favor. The family and friends who had vanished at the first sign of trouble now return to dine with and console him, each bearing a piece of silver and a ring of gold. As for the seven sons and three daughters lost at the start of the story, they are replaced with an identical set of each. Such an exact restoration only God can do.

As one of three sisters, I find it touching that the Bible records the names of Job's new crop of daughters. Millennia later, no one can identify the seven sons who inherited Job's wealth, but Jemimah, Keziah, and Keren-Happuch are remembered whenever the book is read.

The girls' names must have meant something significant to Job, since he is the one who "called" them (42:14). Perhaps with Jemimah ("fair as the day") he remembered how in his opening lament he had cursed the day of his birth and now thanked God for the gift of life. Keziah may have been named for the aromatic herb cassia because Job's flesh was not "caked with worms and dust" (7:5), and nor was his breath "offensive" (19:17) anymore. And Keren-Happuch derives from an ancient Near Eastern box for eye paint. Either Job was grateful his eyelids no longer had "the shadow of death" (16:16), or else the Septuagint's rendering, "Amalthea's horn" meaning "the horn of plenty," is accurate.

Together the names represent Job's fair, fragrant, and full life, and the sisters' beauty is an additional sign of favor. This and the fact that Job "gave them an inheritance among their brothers" (42: 15) suggests he must have had no trouble marrying them off to the most eligible bachelors in Uz.

Apart from the posthumous commendation in Ezekiel 14, God also places Job's name in the New Testament. This lone mention comes from none other than James the brother of the Lord:

> Indeed, we count those blessed who endure. You have heard of the perseverance of Job and seen the end intended by the Lord—that the Lord is very compassionate and merciful. (James 5:11)

Job's story has been included in Scripture as an example; and the one lesson we *must* learn from it is that if we'll persevere in our trials, we will see the outcome intended by the Lord. We can rely on His merciful and compassionate nature and the constancy of His love for us.

In the introduction I had listed the two passages of Scripture I discovered in my crucible of 1993: Psalm 119 and Lamentations 3. In the latter, the prophet Jeremiah expresses his grief over the destruction of Jerusalem in much the same manner that Job had chronicled his woes. For instance, he describes himself as the Lord's "target" (3:12) and the people's "taunting song" (3:14), the very terminology used in Job 16:12 and 30:9.[20]

Just when it looks as though Jeremiah will be lamenting his lot for the rest of this book of lament, he unexpectedly makes one of the most powerful statements in the entire Bible! May it encourage every sufferer as it did me all those years ago.

> Through the LORD's mercies we are not consumed,
> Because His compassions fail not.
> They are new every morning;
> Great is Your faithfulness.
> "The LORD is my portion," says my soul,
> "Therefore I hope in Him!"
> The LORD is good to those who wait for Him,
> To the soul who seeks Him.
> It is good that one should hope and wait quietly
> For the salvation of the LORD. (Lam. 3:22–26)

Appendix: A Letter on Suffering

After the publication of *The Blessing of Melchizedek Devotional* in 2016 Rabi Maharaj, author of *Death of a Guru*, went all out to help with my book promotion efforts. One of the people he put me in touch with was Dr. Miriam Adeney, professor of World Christian Studies at Seattle Pacific University, who graciously agreed to read a review copy. Her email ended with this thought-provoking paragraph:

> *May I ask what is your view about Christian suffering? I agree that God does bless richly those who follow him. Nevertheless, obedient Christians sometimes do experience great suffering. How do you deal with that?*

The following is an excerpt from my reply to Dr. Adeney dated January 29, 2017. I thanked her for wanting to know my views and wrote:

> Most people will agree that suffering is a complex subject, but I believe that blessing is also a complex subject. At least, it isn't as simplistic as "bless me" preaching makes it out to be. Let me summarize my position in three points.

First, I agree that obedient Christians do suffer, and greatly. Church history is full of examples, and believers across the globe are experiencing terrible adversities even right now. Some may never have relief in this life. I myself have certain longstanding physical conditions that have affected other areas of my life. I am not living in willful or conscious disobedience, and I have been praying and believing for healing for years. I cannot be stoical about my sufferings; they are simply too real.

The Bible never promises that we won't have trials. In fact, it promises that we will have trials! But Jesus has also promised every believer His peace in the midst of suffering. Enduring suffering joyfully is a great blessing. And the fact that our Lord has "overcome the world"[1] means we have hope – in this life and especially in the next. I have touched upon trials, the peace of Christ, and the power of His resurrection in *The Blessing of Melchizedek*.

Second, I don't believe that blessing and suffering are mutually exclusive. They can coexist – in the same life and at the same time. A lot has to do with how we view blessing in particular. I write in the very first chapter of my book, "Blessings often come in disguise. They don't always come dressed as themselves."[2] For instance, if distress or lack throws us into worship and God's Word in a deeper way, then it is a blessing – even though distress and lack also qualify as suffering. This is why I say that blessing is not as simplistic as some people believe.

Finally, since we are living in the "now" and the "not yet" of the kingdom of God, we have to deal with life in a city that is not the New Jerusalem. Everybody knows that this world is not perfect, but many Christians are not fully convinced about the reality of the city "whose builder and maker is God."[3] That's why we have so much to learn from Abraham, the dramatic hero of my book.

I don't claim to understand everything about either blessing or suffering, but I hope this gives you some idea of where I'm coming from.

Postscript

The day after I started writing this book on my younger nephew's seventeenth birthday, I decided to transfer the stanzas I had been texting to myself into a notebook. Still propped up in bed with a fever, I reached for a yellow legal pad lying on the bookshelf nearby. As I lifted it, a piece of paper containing these words slid out from underneath:

> *I have written a book on blessing and Miriam Adeney asks what my view of Christian suffering is. This book has emerged out of that email – but it has really emerged out of my life.*

I must have written this right after emailing Dr. Adeney, because the page has the same date: January 29, 2017.

How this loose sheet survived some ruthless paperwork purgings and ended up below the legal pad, I have no idea. But when I read my words from half a decade ago, I immediately thanked God that "this book" never got written. I had so much suffering yet to face—and healing yet to receive—that I could not have done justice to the subject in 2017.

As I held the sheet of paper, marveling at how it had resurfaced so opportunely, a warm, tingling sensation unexpectedly engulfed the upper part of my body. My sufferings flashed before me in an instant, but instead of sorrow and despair a strong, steady hope filled my being. Deep within, I sensed the Holy Spirit assuring me that every painful moment I had endured, even in the agonizing months since my mother's death, had been preparing me for such a time as this.

When the sensation subsided and a quiet confidence settled upon me, I wrote a brief postscript under my note from 2017 and placed the paper at the back of my journal for safekeeping. Then I picked up a pencil, leaned forward as I had done while composing my first poem at the age of six, and began to write.

Endnotes

INTRODUCTION

1. Originally published in *Light of Life* magazine, Mumbai, September 1994. Used with permission.

AFTERWORD

1. The day after I met Vinoth on Gorai Beach, it struck me that he would make a perfect match for my Danish friend, Karin Lautrup. I lent her my copy of *Gods That Fail*, hoping it would win her heart. She read it quickly, dissected it in a way I could only dumbly admire, and they were married the following year. Karin sadly lost her battle with cancer some months shy of their twentieth wedding anniversary in 2018. Though she was one of the bravest people I have known, such is physical pain that even Karin prayed she would go peacefully in her sleep.

2. In his classic work on the subject, C. S. Lewis sets the problem of pain in terms of God's character:

   'If God were good, He would wish to make His creatures perfectly happy, and if God were almighty He would be able to do what He wishes. But the creatures are not happy. Therefore God lacks either goodness, or power, or both.' This is the problem of pain, in its simplest form. (*The Problem of Pain* [New York: Harper Collins, 2001, orig. pub. 1940], 16)

3. The truth that God is with us is reflected throughout Scripture, including in the name Immanuel, which appears in the very first chapter of the New Testament. After quoting the prophecy in Isaiah 7:14—"*Behold, the virgin shall be with child, and bear a Son, and they shall call His name Immanuel*"—Matthew adds the name's translation: "God with us" (1:23). And he ends his Gospel with Christ's famous promise, "I am with you always, even to the end of the age" (28:20). After a lifetime of singleness I can confidently say that one of the best things to remind ourselves of when we are suffering is that *God is with us*.

4. Writes the 17th-century French mystic we call Madame Guyon:

> Yours is a God who often hides Himself. He hides Himself for a purpose. Why? *His purpose is to rouse you from spiritual laziness.* His purpose in removing Himself from you is to cause you to pursue Him. (Jeanne Guyon, *Experiencing the Depths of Jesus Christ* [Sargent, GA: SeedSowers, 1975], 27. Italics in original)

5. God can use people to deliver His word to us, of course, but they are merely messengers. If the message itself is of human origin, it will at best cheer us momentarily. Only God's words have the power to change our hearts, renew our minds and, at His appointed time, transform our circumstances.

6. *Merriam-Webster's Collegiate Dictionary*, 11th ed. (Springfield, MA: Merriam-Webster, 2005), s.v. "Job's comforter."

7. Job's friends certainly come across as his foes once they begin speaking, but the book's opening chapters leave us in no doubt as to the real enemy. Nowhere else in Scripture do we see Satan so clearly depicted in his role as "the accuser of the brethren" (Rev. 12:10). Philip Yancey makes this insightful observation about the adversary's bid to destroy Job:

> In the first two chapters of Job, Satan reveals himself as the first great behaviorist. He claimed that faith is merely a product of environment and circumstances. Job was *conditioned* to love God. Take away the positive rewards, Satan challenged, and watch Job's faith crumble. Poor Job, oblivious, was selected for the cosmic contest to determine this

crucial matter of human freedom. (*Where Is God When It Hurts?* Anniversary ed. [Grand Rapids, MI: Zondervan, 2002, orig. pub. 1977], 89–90. Italics in original)

8. Early in his opening speech Eliphaz, the first of Job's friends to speak, refers to Job's integrity by asking, "Is not . . . the integrity of your ways your hope?" (4:6). This is before Eliphaz and company forget about their friend's integrity and begin accusing him of iniquity. We, who know the full story, prize Job's integrity more highly. As Charles R. Swindoll says:

> In spite of all the hardship and loss, regardless of insults, false accusations, and condemning put-downs, he never compromised his integrity. Suffering we admire, and the endurance of intensified suffering we admire even more. But the modeling of integrity through it all—we stand in admiration of that. *Nothing about Job is more impressive. (Job: A Man of Heroic Endurance* [Nashville, TN: Thomas Nelson, 2004], 232. Italics added)

9. With respect to Satan's brazen accusation of Job, the theologian John Edgar McFadyen wrote:

> In casting doubt upon the sincerity of Job, Satan was also implicitly denying the lovableness of God: a man might love God for what He gave, but not conceivably for what He was. Thus God was on His trial, no less than Job. (*The Problem of Pain: A Study in the Book of Job* [London: James Clarke & Co., c. 1910], 17)

10. The *mot juste* for Elihu may be insufferable, but my penchant for alliteration induced me to use enigmatic in this section's title. When I discovered Swindoll's book while editing one of the later drafts, I was amused to learn that he considers "enigma" a good word for Elihu. *Job*, 252.

11. The Hebrew word often translated understanding, *bin*, appears over 80 times in the Wisdom books, including 23 times in Job and 33 times in Proverbs. The Bible's longest chapter, Psalm 119, contains ten instances of *bin*, in verses 27, 34, 73, 95, 100, 104, 125, 130, 144, and 169. James Strong, *The New Strong's*

Complete Dictionary of Bible Words (Nashville, TN: Thomas Nelson, 1996; orig. pub. 1890), s.v. "bin" (H995).

12. The fear of the Lord is mentioned in the Bible's other Wisdom books as well. See Psalms 19:9, 111:10; Proverbs 1:7, 2:2–6, 9:10, 14:26–27, 15:33; and Ecclesiastes 12:13.

13. Sharon Edwards, *Pioneer Boulevard* (Los Angeles: Consonant Books, 2013), 47–48. Italics added.

14. How much Job knew about the death and resurrection of his Redeemer we will find out only in eternity, but we who call Christ our Redeemer must believe in His bodily resurrection. In the "resurrection chapter" of 1 Corinthians, the apostle Paul asserts that if Christ did not rise from the dead, our faith is "futile" and we are still in our sins (15:17). If our hope is for this life only, he adds, then we are of all people "the most pitiable" (15:19). In my previous book, these two verses immediately follow this passage on the centrality of our Lord's resurrection:

> Everything stands or falls on whether we believe that Jesus rose from the dead. It is not enough to believe that He was born of a virgin, that He lived a sinless life, and that He performed many miracles. It is not even enough to believe that He suffered on the cross for our sins. Unless we believe that He died and *vanquished death by rising again*, our faith is not of eternal value. (*The Blessing of Melchizedek Devotional* [Los Angeles: Consonant Books, 2016], 100. Italics in original)

15. Strong, *Complete Dictionary*, s.v. "nacham" (H5162). The seven times this word appears in Job are 2:11, 7:13, 16:2, 21:34, 29:25, 42:6, and 42:11.

16. Even though he suffered innocently and never cursed God, Job rightly saw his need to repent, for at times he had spoken of the Lord as though He were not good. Moreover, in his anguish he had cursed his own life, that precious first gift from God, and had fallen into a self-pity unworthy of a servant of God (e.g., 3:3–11, 7:11, 10:1). As Paul E. Billheimer points out,

God testified that Job was a holy man, yet there were traits of self-centeredness of which, at first, he was totally unaware and which could be spotlighted and removed only by deep affliction. (*Don't Waste Your Sorrows* [Secunderabad, India: Authentic Books, 2013, orig. pub. 1977], 94)

17. Vinoth Ramachandra, *Gods That Fail*, rev. ed. (Eugene, OR: Wipf & Stock, 2016), 67–68.

18. The poem quoted in the introduction, "Care," is based on Matthew 6:25–34, but its title was inspired by the wordplay in 1 Peter 5:7, "Casting all your care upon Him, for He cares for you." The Lord's care is beautifully lauded in Robert Grant's best-known hymn, "O Worship the King":

Thy bountiful care, what tongue can recite?
It breathes in the air, it shines in the light.
It streams from the hills, it descends to the plain,
And sweetly distills in the dew and the rain.

This is among my favorite hymns, and I feel an affinity with the hymnist because of his Indian connection. Born in Bengal in 1779, when the East India Company ruled the land, the young Robert moved to England in 1790. He studied at Cambridge and enjoyed success as a lawyer and parliamentarian before being knighted and appointed Governor of Bombay in 1834. Mumbai's historic Grant Medical College is named for him, as is Grant Road Station. I was living with my parents in this bustling locality when I read Job for the first time as an adult. Grant died in 1838 near my hometown of Pune. The church where his remains are housed is affiliated with my alma mater, St. Mary's School. It was here that I discovered, at the ripe age of six, the wonders of reading, writing, and poetry.

19. Theodore H. Epp, *Why Do Christians Suffer?* (Lincoln, NE: Back to the Bible, 1970), 80.

20. Jeremiah may have had reason to refer to himself as God's "target" (Lam. 3:12), since as a prophet he identified with his people, who were being judged for their sin through the destruction of Jerusalem. But Job was Satan's target, not God's. When the Lord asks Satan if he has "considered" His servant Job (1:8, 2:3), the

Hebrew literally means "set your heart on." This implies that Satan had already marked Job as a target prior to appearing before God, and our upright hero was wrong in assuming that God was behind his suffering.

APPENDIX

1. The quoted phrase appears in the second sentence of John 16:33, where Jesus says, "In this world you will have tribulation, but be of good cheer, for I have overcome the world." This truth has strengthened me in many a trial.

2. *Melchizedek Devotional*, 20.

3. This phrase is taken from Hebrews 11:10, a verse I had quoted on Day 63 of my devotional:

> Today we know that Abraham's alien status had spiritual significance, not least because it reflected his great faith. As we are told in the Bible's faith chapter,
>
>> By faith he dwelt in the land of promise as in a foreign country, dwelling in tents with Isaac and Jacob, the heirs with him of the same promise; for he waited for the city which has foundations, whose builder and maker is God. (Heb. 11:9–10)
>
> Like the patriarchs, we are to dwell in this world *as in a foreign country*, because as citizens of the kingdom of God, this world *is* a foreign country. Its systems and values are contrary to those of the kingdom of God. Whether we live in the place where we were born and raised or in a country or culture that is foreign to us, we are to live in this world as "aliens and strangers" (1 Pet. 2:11). *Melchizedek Devotional*, 143. Italics in original.

Acknowledgements

I begin by thanking God for Irwin and Lalita Edwards, who gave me, with life and other good things, the gift of faith and poetry. As my parents, they were also the first to give me the gift of suffering. I once was blind, but now I now see it for the gift it was. I must remember to thank them when we meet again on the other side.

My sisters and their families have been a source of deep comfort since Mummy left us in May 2021. Special thanks to my older sister for her godly counsel in the months following our loss; and to my youngest niece for a delightful text about poetry five days after I began this book. "Today I decided to read this old book that belonged to you," she wrote, referring to *Poems of Shelley*. She had attached images of the frontispiece and those lovely opening lines of "The Cloud":

> I bring fresh showers to thirsting flowers
>> From the seas and the streams;
> I bear light shade for the leaves when laid
>> In their noonday dreams.

For that text, Samaya was the first to know I had written a book of poetry. It's my great joy to dedicate it to all five of my nephews and nieces with my blessings, prayers, and love.

I must again thank Vinoth Ramachandra for that copy of *Gods That Fail*, which inspired me to read the Book of Job for the first time as an adult. I likewise appreciate his encouraging feedback on the afterword.

In her email of January 29, 2017, Dr. Miriam Adeney asked me a question that prompted me to consider writing a book on suffering. It has turned out to be very different from the one I outlined that day, but I am indebted to Dr. Adeney for planting the seed.

Belated thanks to *Light of Life* magazine, Mumbai, for debuting me as a Christian poet with the publication of "Care" in September 1994. I appreciate the permission to reprint it here.

I am grateful beyond words to the dear relatives and friends who upheld me in prayer and rendered all manner of practical help as I wrote this book. Many of them, including my goddaughter, Alita Sharon, were kind enough to also lend me their ears as I read or recited my limericks. May their tribe increase!

My sincerest thanks to the two gentlemen (not of Verona) who braved early drafts of the introduction and did unto me what I have done to others as an editor. In my book, this is not payback but *back pay*.

A big *dhanyavaad* to Rabi Maharaj for his efforts to promote my previous books and his enthusiasm for this one. May it go as far and wide as *Death of a Guru*.

I remain indebted to Dr. G. Walter Hansen, my New Testament professor at seminary, for shaping me as a scholar and a writer twenty years ago. Even though this book is based on the Old Testament, I wrote with that prized "A!" in mind.

I bless God for the spiritual leaders He brought into my life at various points, people who prayed for me and gave me biblical counsel in my sundry trials. In particular I wish to acknowledge

Pastors Ché Ahn, Dale Turner, Ivan Raskino, Michael Koh, and Raju Thomas. This book's epilogue has been influenced to some extent by each of them.

I owe *yashar* Job a debt I will never be able to repay this side of eternity. Had he cursed God and died instead of enduring his suffering, I would not have had the indescribable joy of learning from his life and writing my own book on the problem of pain. For his example of perseverance, and his posthumous part in the biggest surprise of my life, I look forward to thanking him face-to-face someday.

With words that fall woefully short, I pour out my heart's deepest gratitude to the One who is worthy of it all.

Father God, thank you for loving me my whole life, even in the womb.

Holy Spirit, thank you for giving me the idea for this book, amongst innumerable gifts of grace.

And Lord Jesus, theme of my soul's best songs, thank you for suffering for me and with me. Maranatha.